THEMES
FROM A
LETTER
TO
ROME

THEMES FROM A LETTER TO
ROME

Daniel L. Segraves

Themes from a Letter to Rome

by Daniel L. Segraves

ISBN 1-56722-136-X

©1995, Word Aflame Press
Hazelwood, MO 63042-2299

Cover design by Paul Povolni

Printed in United States of America

Printed by

Contents

Preface

Although the Book of Romans is not the earliest New Testament letter to be written (that distinction belongs to James, written perhaps as early as A.D. 47-48) or even the earliest letter written by Paul (Paul's first letter was Galatians, written about A.D. 49), it is fitting that Romans should be the first in order among the Epistles. The central message of Romans—justification by faith—is foundational and essential for understanding all that follows in the other letters. Leon Tucker has pointed out that until we know the "righteousness of Romans," we cannot move on to the "order of Corinthians," the "liberty of Galatians," the "calling of Ephesians," the "joy of Philippians," the "head of Colossians," the "coming One of Thessalonians," or the "substance of Hebrews."[1]

Actually, justification by faith is not the only major theme in this letter to the believers at Rome. At least seven major topics occupied Paul's thoughts as he penned these words. A parallel theme to justification is righteousness; both words spring from the same Greek root. In addition to righteousness/justification and faith, the letter extensively discusses law, grace, and holiness. Throughout the book, we can also trace the dealings of God with the nation of Israel and with Gentiles.

To expand on Leon Tucker's observation, we can say that without a grasp of the predominant motifs found in Paul's letter to the Romans, much of the epistolary literature of the New Testament will be difficult to understand. All the letters to the church deal in some way with these themes.

Peter wrote, concerning Paul's letters, "In them . . . are some things hard to understand, which those who are untaught and unstable twist to their own destruction, as they do also the rest of the Scriptures" (II Peter 3:16). The specific topic Peter had in mind was salvation. (See II Peter 3:15.) In the broadest sense, salvation is the topic of Romans.

We might expect, then, as Peter testified, that there would be some things in this letter "hard to understand." But we must not allow that to deter us from exercising all diligence in our attempt to grasp its content. Peter did not mean to discourage believers from studying Paul's letters. After all, Peter recognized the letters of Paul as Scripture and as worthy of careful study and obedience as the writings of the Hebrew prophets. (See II Peter 3:2.) On the other hand, we must take Peter's warning seriously: to twist Paul's message is destructive. The proper response to Peter's caution is not to abandon Paul's letters; it is to pursue the accurate teaching and stability of character that will enable us to understand Paul's message correctly.

Competent critics have never questioned the validity of the Book of Romans. From the most ancient times Christians have uniformly accepted its authorship, genuineness, and inspiration. Though three ancient heretical sects called the letter into question, it was because they could not harmonize its doctrines with their views. Even they did not question the Pauline authorship of Romans. These groups were the Ebionites, who believed in the humanity but not the deity of Jesus; the Encratites, Gnostic ascetics who abstained from eating meat, drinking wine and marriage; and Cerinthians, professing Christians who denied the virgin birth of Jesus.

Romans provides a solid foundation in New Testament soteriology, the doctrine of salvation. The letter reveals that since all humans are sinners who cannot earn or deserve salvation, God has provided salvation as a free gift. Though the nation of Israel failed to keep the covenant God had made with them at Sinai and are presently rejected as a nation, God will graciously and freely provide national salvation for them in the future. And Romans reveals that genuine Christianity will result in practical expressions of faith in one's life.

Note
[1]Leon Tucker, quoted in C. W. Slemming, *The Bible Digest* (Grand Rapids, MI: Kregel Publications, 1960), 650.

Righteousness and Justification: Imputing Right Standing to the Believer's Account

Some contemporary theologians have referred to the doctrine of justification by faith as a "theological dinosaur."[1] If pressed, we might have to agree that many believers do not have a firm grasp of the meaning of justification or, for that matter, righteousness. But the fault is not with the doctrine or its relevance to modern man. The human race at the turn of the twenty-first century is as desperately in need of the good news contained in the doctrine of justification by faith as ever. At least part of the problem may be that some preachers and teachers have largely abandoned the doctrine, apparently in favor of topics they perceive to be more exciting or immediately rewarding.

But in a world that trembles on the brink of self-destruction, pushed ever closer to irretrievable disaster by the plague of meaninglessness and despair, there is a desperate need for the church to declare boldly and clearly the marvelous news that people can find meaning and hope by accepting the free gift of God. If we were able to erase the technological differences, would there really be that much difference between our day and Paul's? Life in the first century, dominated by the Roman Empire, had its share of violence, deception, poverty, moral impurity, and hopelessness. Into that world came the apostle Paul, not with a frothy message of social reform, not with pop psychology's formulas for self-improvement, but with the solid truth that by faith in God, it is possible to find meaning, purpose, and hope. By faith in God, it is possible that the righteousness of Jesus Christ, the Messiah, can be placed on one's eternal record, just as the sins of the world have been placed on His. (See II Corinthians 5:21.)

The word *righteous* comes from the old English word *rightwise*. It has to do with being right, or being in right relationship with someone. It is thus precisely the correct word to translate the concept from the Hebrew and Greek languages.

The Book of Romans uses six Greek words, translated by ten English words or phrases in the King James Version (KJV), to describe some aspect of the righteousness of God. These Greek words are *dikaiosune*, *dikaioma*, *dikaiosis*, *dikaiokrisia*, *dikaios*, and *dikaioo*. All of these spring from the same root, *dike*, which finds its origin in *deiknuo*, which in turn means "to point out, to show, to make known."[2] *Dike* originally meant "direction, way," and it was used during the eighth through the sixth centuries before Christ to describe "what is right."[3] In Romans, the KJV translates these words as follows: "righteousness, judgment, justification, righteous judgment, just, justified, justifier, justify, justifieth, and freed."

In the New Testament, then, the verb "to justify" (Greek *dikaioo*) is built on the same root as "righteous" (Greek *dikaios*) and "righteousness" (Greek *dikaiosune*). The idea expressed by *dikaioo* is "to *declare* righteous," not "to *make* righteous."[4]

The teaching on justification in Paul's writings reflects the Old Testament background of the theme. Righteousness in the Old Testament (Hebrew *tsedeq* and *tsedaqa*) has to do with conforming to a given norm.[5] The use of the word is wide ranging, referring even to conformity to the norms demanded by family relationships.[6]

Essentially, righteousness is a concept of relationship.[7] "The righteous man is he who in God's judgment meets the divine standard and thus stands in a right relationship with God."[8]

Frequently the idea of righteousness is understood in a forensic or legal context: "the righteous man is he whom the judge declares to be free from guilt."[9]

In New Testament times, however, the Jewish idea of righteousness was based on "the merit of good works."[10] If, at the end of a day, a person's good deeds outweighed his bad deeds, he was considered righteous or justified. At the final judgment, all a person's deeds would be tallied up, and if his good works outweighed his bad, he would be justified.

While some theologians, notably Roman Catholics, have held that the work of justification actually imparts righteousness to the individual, the New Testament teaches not that justification is an impartation of righteousness, but the restoration of relationship with God.[11]

13

When compared with first-century Jewish theology, the startling news about this Christian view was the declaration that the ungodly are justified in Christ: "But to him that worketh not, but believeth on him that justifieth the ungodly, his faith is counted for righteousness" (Romans 4:5, KJV). In further contrast to the Jewish idea, the New Testament asserts that this justification has nothing to do with the works of the law; it is by faith alone: "Knowing that a man is not justified by the works of the law, but by the faith of Jesus Christ, even we have believed in Jesus Christ, that we might be justified by the faith of Christ, and not by the works of the law: for by the works of the law shall no flesh be justified. . . . But that no man is justified by the law in the sight of God, it is evident: for, The just shall live by faith" (Galatians 2:16; 3:11, KJV).

In the interest of making this central doctrine relevant to people on the eve of the twenty-first century, and since righteousness/justification is primarily relational, it has been suggested that a more helpful translation than "justified" would be "right with God."[12] This restoration to fellowship with God, destroyed in the Garden of Eden, is made possible by the death and resurrection of Jesus Christ:

"Being justified freely by his grace through the redemption that is in Christ Jesus: whom God hath set forth to be a propitiation through faith in his blood, to declare his righteousness for the remission of sins that are past, through the forbearance of God; to declare, I say, at this time his righteousness: that he might be just, and the justifier of him which believeth in Jesus" *(Romans 3:24-26, KJV).*

"*But for us also, to whom it shall be imputed, if we believe on him that raised up Jesus our Lord from the dead; who was delivered for our offences, and was raised again for our justification*" *(Romans 4:24-25, KJV).*

"*Much more then, being now justified by his blood, we shall be saved from wrath through him*" *(Romans 5:9, KJV).*

In these and related passages, the righteousness of God is twofold: "a *gift from God*" and "*the transforming power of God.*"[13]

Justification involves an exchange between Christ and the believer: "For he hath made him to be sin for us, who knew no sin; that we might be made the righteousness of God in him" (II Corinthians 5:21, KJV). While Christ Himself never sinned, He was somehow made "to be sin" on behalf of the believer, so that those who had never been righteous "might be made the righteousness of God."

The Gospel Reveals the Righteousness of God

The first time the Epistle to the Romans addresses the subject of righteousness it declares that the righteousness of God is revealed in the gospel of Christ: "For I am not ashamed of the gospel of Christ, for it is the power of God to salvation for everyone who believes, for the Jew first and also for the Greek. For in it the righteousness of God is revealed from faith to faith; as it is written, 'The just shall live by faith'" (Romans 1:16-17). God has made provision for people to return to right relationship with Him by means of the gospel of Christ.

The gospel is the good news that Christ died for our sins, was buried, and rose again on the third day (I Corinthians 15:1-4). The substitutionary death of Jesus Christ for our sins and His subsequent resurrection is what gives meaning to the Christian faith (I Corinthians 15:14, 17, 20-23). His resurrection provides the assurance that all who have placed their trust in His work on their behalf on Calvary's cross will be united with Him in His life (I Corinthians 15:49, 51-57).

Hearing and Doing

The law of Moses did not offer justification to those who merely heard what the law had to say, or even to those who may have mentally agreed with the law. "For not the hearers of the law are just in the sight of God, but the doers of the law will be justified" (Romans 2:13). The law promised justification only to those who perfectly obeyed the law ("doers"). Although the law contained 613 commandments, it was one unit, one covenant. It was not sufficient to keep most of the commandments most of the time, or even ninety-five percent of them all of the time. To break just one commandment was to break the entire law. (See James 2:10.)

Some Jews boasted that they were special people because they had been given the law, but the law by definition was a system of condemnation because it demanded the impossible: perfect obedience. Elsewhere, Paul referred to the law of Moses as "the letter" that "kills," "the ministry of death," and the "ministry of condemnation" (II Corinthians 3:6-9).

The New Testament explains the radical differences between the old covenant (the law of Moses) and the new covenant. (See Romans, II Corinthians, Galatians, Philippians, and Colossians.) The Book of Hebrews is totally given to the theme that the new covenant, which is better in every way, has replaced the old covenant.

The two covenants are different in their purpose, their requirements, their benefits, and their basis. The old covenant was an earth-bound covenant given exclusively to the nation of Israel. Its promises had to do exclusively with temporal life on earth, and specifically life in the tiny plot of earth known as Israel. The old covenant was given to no other nation than Israel (Psalm 147:20). It promised earthly prosperity and health. Though the promised benefits of the old covenant were marvelous, there was one major drawback: The requirement to receive all the promises was perfect obedience to all 613 commandments of the law of Moses (e.g., Deuteronomy 28:1).

The old covenant was a temporary covenant given at Mt. Sinai and meant to extend only until the coming of the promised Messiah (Romans 10:4; Galatians 3:19). We can identify several purposes of the law, but the essential purpose was to serve as a disciplinarian over the nation of Israel until the Messiah came (Galatians 3:23-24). After Messiah came, Israel was no longer under the law (Galatians 3:25).

God intended that the perfect standard required by the law would demonstrate to Israel the need for a Messiah to deliver them from their sins. From Sinai to the coming of Jesus, Israel should have seen, generation after generation, the impossibility of measuring up to the standard of perfection required by the law. This should have caused them to cry out to God for their Messiah.

Instead, many Israelites came to view the law as the end in itself, rather than the means to an end. They attempted to achieve righteousness by the works of the law rather than by faith, and thus they stumbled at Christ's teaching that righteousness comes only on the basis of faith in Him. (See Romans 9:30-33; 10:1-13.)

The justification available on the basis of the works of the law was not soteriological (i.e., it did not produce salvation), but relational (i.e., it had to do with one's relationship with one's fellow man [e.g., Deuteronomy 24:13]). Indeed, the law of Moses did not provide soteriological (salvific) righteousness. (See Acts 13:39; Galatians 3:21.) Paul declared that prior to his conversion to Christ, he was blameless "concerning the righteousness which is in the law" (Philippians 3:6), but that the righteousness which is from the law is self-righteousness (Philippians 3:9).

It might be protested that Paul's understanding of the law prior to his conversion was a perversion, but he denied that idea. Long after he became a Christian, as he defended himself at the Temple in Jerusalem, Paul proclaimed, "I am verily a man which am a Jew, born in Tarsus, a city in Cilicia, yet brought up in this city at the feet of Gamaliel, and taught according to the perfect manner of the law of the fathers, and was zealous toward God, as ye all are this day" (Acts 22:3, KJV).

The statement that the commandment "was to bring life" (Romans 7:10) is informed by such passages as Deuteronomy 30:15-20, where the life promised by the law is clearly life in the land promised to Abraham, Isaac, and Jacob. The life promised for obedience to the commandments of the law in Leviticus 18:5 is defined contextually as life in the Promised Land. The Lord brought Israel to the land of Canaan to allow them to live in it, as He had promised the patriarchs, but if they engaged in the immoral sins described in the chapter, the land would vomit them out as it had its inhabitants before them. (See Leviticus 18:3, 24-29.) Disobedient people would be "cut off from among their people" by being cast out of the land (Leviticus 18:29).

This is not to suggest that no one was saved during the era of the law of Moses, or that the Jewish people who lived under the Sinaitic covenant were unaware of the concept of eternal life. People of faith were saved from sin and received the gift of eternal life during the law just as they have during every age, by grace through faith. (See Habakkuk 2:4; Ephesians 2:8-9; Hebrews 11.) Noah and Job, who lived prior to the law of Moses, shared in the same righteousness as Daniel, who lived under the law. (See Ezekiel 14:14, 20.)

The point is that God never intended the law of Moses to provide salvation. Its purpose was not soteriological. (See Galatians 3:21.) Instead, it was intended, among other things, to govern the life of Israel in the Promised Land until the coming of the Messiah. The Abrahamic covenant, with its blessing of justification by faith, was still in effect when the law was given, and the covenant given at Sinai could add no conditions to that. (See Galatians 3:7-9, 13-18.)

On the other hand, the new covenant, established in Christ's blood rather than in the blood of bulls and goats (Matthew 26:28; Hebrews 10:4), offers eternal life on the basis of faith (John 3:16). It makes no requirement of obedience to the legal code given at Sinai.

Can the Uncircumcised Be Righteous?

No doubt Paul's Jewish readers in Rome were shocked when they read, "Therefore, if an uncircumcised man keeps the righteous requirements of the law, will not his uncircumcision be counted as circumcision?" (Romans 2:26).

Abraham was accounted righteous before he was circumcised (Romans 4:3, 9-10), on the basis of his faith in God alone. For him, circumcision was a seal, a validation, of the righteousness he already possessed (Romans 4:11). Abraham was not accounted righteous because he was circumcised; he was circumcised because he had already been accounted righteous. This was so Abraham could be considered "the father of all those who believe" (Romans 4:11), whether they were Gentile (uncircumcised) or Jew (circumcised) (Romans 4:12).

Since Abraham was accounted righteous prior to circumcision, any Gentile could be accounted righteous apart from circumcision if he had the kind of faith Abraham had (Romans 4:12). Jews could not be accounted righteous on the basis of circumcision alone; they also had to have the kind of faith possessed by Abraham to be accounted righteous (Romans 4:12).

This information from the life of Abraham before his circumcision assists in understanding Romans 2:26. If a Gentile, who by definition was uncircumcised, kept the commandments of the law, his lack of circumcision would not keep him from receiving God's approval (Romans 2:29).

This is apparently an hypothetical observation. No Gentile actually did keep the law of Moses perfectly, for all people, Jews and Gentiles, are sinners who continually fall short of God's glorious standard of perfection (Romans 3:23). The point is that *if* a Gentile were to keep the law, no Jew could legitimately claim to be superior to that Gentile. That the Jew was circumcised and the Gentile was not would not make the Jew a better person. In short, "there is no partiality with God" (Romans 2:11). No physical characteristic (like circumcision) makes one person better than another.

God Will Be Justified

Romans uses the strongest possible Greek term to deny that the unfaithfulness of some in Israel could negate God's faithfulness. In answer to the question, "Will their unbelief make the faithfulness of God without effect?" (Romans 3:3), Paul wrote under inspiration, "Certainly not! Indeed, let God be true but every man a liar. As it is written: 'That You may be justified in Your words, and may overcome when You are judged'" (Romans 3:4). The term *me genoito* is somewhat difficult to translate into English. The KJV renders it, "God forbid." The NKJV translates it, "Certainly not!" *Me* is the negative particle; *genoito* is from a word meaning "to be." A literal translation is, "May it never be."

The passage reinforces the impossibility of human unfaithfulness negating God's faithfulness by continuing, "Indeed, let God be true but every man a liar." Even if all people are unfaithful, it will not change God. God keeps His word on every count, regardless of circumstances.

To further deny the proposition that human unfaithfulness will negate God's faithfulness, Paul quoted from the Septuagint translation of Psalm 51:4. The point of this quote is that no one will ever be able to accuse God of injustice or unfaithfulness. When people stand before God in judgment, they will be speechless, for it will be clear and evident that the judgment He pronounces is precisely according to the facts in each person's life. (See Revelation 20:12-13.) As Romans 3:19 puts it, the unfaithfulness of man as contrasted to the faithfulness of God results in "every mouth" being "stopped."

Universal Unrighteousness

Romans 3:10 begins a series of quotations from the Old Testament to prove that all are sinners. The first quote is from Psalm 14:1-3. It eliminates the possibility of anyone claiming to be righteous, to have understanding, to seek after God, to refrain from sin, to be a profitable servant of God, or to do good. (See also Ecclesiastes 7:20.) Though not stated here, we learn elsewhere that if any of these good things are present in a person's life, they are the direct result of the grace of God at work. (See Philippians 2:13.) Thus, no person can claim credit for them, nor can he claim moral or ethnic superiority over others because of them. All praise must go to God. (See Romans 3:27.)

The Righteousness of God Versus the Unrighteousness of Men

The inherent unrighteousness of human beings serves only to demonstrate all the more clearly the righteousness of God. "But if our unrighteousness demonstrates the righteousness of God, what shall we say? Is God unjust who inflicts wrath? (I speak as a man.)" (Romans 3:5). Just as light shines brighter the darker the night, the righteousness of God shines even more brilliantly when compared with the darkness of human unrighteousness.

To some, then, it may seem that people should be encouraged to greater wickedness, so as to display the righteousness of God even more clearly. "And why not say, 'Let us do evil that good may come'?" (Romans 3:8a). But this is human reasoning. Another human question would be, "If sin only demonstrates the righteousness of God, how can it be fair for God to judge me for something that only proves His goodness?" Human reasoning suggests, "God should be happy I'm a sinner; it only proves that He is not!" Or, "The worse I am, the better God looks, so He should be glad I'm so bad!"

Like Romans 3:4, Romans 3:6 responds to this faulty reasoning with the strong term, *me genoito*, or "Certainly not!" If humans are to be as evil as possible in order to put God in a better light, God would have no basis upon which to pronounce judgment upon the sinful world. There would be no need to fear God. Taken to its logical conclusion, people would be actively encouraged to murder, to steal, to be dishonest, and to commit every form of violent, perverse behavior (Romans 3:6).

Still using human reasoning, Paul asked, "If, when I lie, it demonstrates more clearly how truthful God is and thus brings glory to Him, why does He still judge me as being a sinner?" (See Romans 3:7.) Shouldn't God rejoice in our sinfulness? As strange as it may seem, some slandered Paul by claiming he actually taught that people should engage in evil in order to bring glory to God. But those who misrepresented him in this way would be justly condemned (Romans 3:8). Though human sinfulness does indeed demonstrate the righteousness of God, the proper response is not to indulge in greater evil, but to accept the free gift of right standing with God.

No Justification by the Law

Romans 3:20 declares a theme reiterated elsewhere: No one will be justified before God by the works of the law. "Therefore by the deeds of the law no flesh will be justified in His sight, for by the law is the knowledge of sin." (See also Acts 13:39; Galatians 2:16; 3:21; Romans 3:28; 4:5.) The reason is that God did not give the law of Moses to provide a means of salvific justification; He gave it to define sin to Israel. (See Romans 7:7.) The law did not create sin; people were sinners already. But the law did define the sins already in their hearts.

Righteousness Apart from the Law

The righteousness discussed in the Book of Romans is not connected to the law of Moses. The law of Moses was terminated as an active covenant and replaced by the new covenant. "But now the righteousness of God apart from the law is revealed, being witnessed by the Law and the prophets" (Romans 3:21).

This statement came as a shocking revelation to Jewish readers; the idea that the righteousness of God could exist *apart from the law* was incredible to them.[14] Even more surprising to them was the idea that the Hebrew Scriptures themselves foretold of a time when this would be true. (See Romans 1:2; 3:1.) The Hebrew Scriptures predicted the coming of the new covenant and the necessary passing away of the old covenant. This new covenant is by definition something "apart from the law." It is not merely a further development of the law, or another form of the same covenant; it is a different covenant altogether, so radically different from the law of Moses as to be "apart" from the law.

Righteousness through Faith

The righteousness of God is "through faith in Jesus Christ, to all and on all who believe. For there is no difference" (Romans 3:22). "The righteousness of God" has to do with the plan of God to bring people into right relationship with Him. Under the new covenant, people enter into a right relationship with God on the basis of their faith (trust, reliance) in Jesus Christ.

The new covenant is a faith covenant; the old covenant was based on works.[15] (See Romans 10:5; Galatians 3:12.) There is nothing in the new covenant of the sacrificial system, of the Tabernacle or Temple, of holy days, or the other requirements of the law of Moses. Whereas the law of Moses focused on an elaborate system of rituals, the new covenant focuses on a person: Jesus Christ.

The righteousness of God introduced by the new covenant is available "to all and on all who believe." The distinction between Jew and Gentile is irrelevant under the new covenant: "there is no difference." (See also Galatians 3:28.) In context, this statement is designed to show Jews the error of any claim of superiority over the Gentiles. Ethnic origin has no bearing on new covenant salvation; faith is the determining factor.

Justified by His Grace

After establishing the universal sinfulness of humanity, Romans describes the means by which people may come into right standing with God. In the simplest terms, it is by faith in Jesus Christ. Since this is true, Jews have no legitimate reason to boast in the law of Moses; it is not the means of justification. Abraham and David are examples of men of faith who were justified by faith, not by works (Romans 4:1-8).

In contrast to the law of Moses with its demand for perfection, the new covenant provides for those who have faith in Jesus Christ to be "justified freely by His [God's] grace through the redemption that is in Christ Jesus" (Romans 3:24). Justification refers to the right standing with God that Jesus possesses, which is credited to the believer's account. It is not something that is earned by performance; it is freely given. By definition, justification is a gift; the recipient of justification does not deserve his new status.

In other words, justification comes by the grace of God. Though the full theological meaning of grace extends beyond merely "the unmerited favor of God," it certainly does include that idea. The word translated "grace" is from the Greek *charis*, which has to do with a free gift.

The basis upon which this free gift of justification is given is "the redemption that is in Christ Jesus." The word translated "redemption" is from the Greek *lutroo*, which means to loose or set free. (The same root word is used in Luke 1:68; 2:38; 21:28; 24:21; Romans 3:24; I Corinthians 1:30; Ephesians 1:7, 14; 4:30; Colossians 1:14; Titus 2:14; Hebrews 9:12, 15; I Peter 1:18.) Other Greek words used in the New Testament to describe various aspects of redemption include *agorazo*, which means to buy in the market (I Corinthians 6:20; 7:23; II Peter 2:1; Revelation 5:9; 14:3-4), and *exagorazo*, which means to buy out of the market, or to purchase and remove from further sale

(Galatians 3:13; 4:5; Ephesians 5:16; Colossians 4:5).

In this case, the redemption provided by Christ Jesus sets the believer free from the law of sin and death, or the law of Moses. (See Romans 8:2-3.) The law of Moses was the law of sin and death in that it identified sin (Romans 7:7) and prescribed death for the violation of its commandments (Romans 6:23). The redemption provided in the new covenant is not in the law of Moses or any system of regulations; it is in the person of Christ Jesus.

Righteousness and Propitiation

Romans 3:25-26 states, concerning Christ Jesus, "Whom God set forth to be a propitiation by His blood, through faith, to demonstrate His righteousness, because in His forbearance God had passed over the sins that were previously committed, to demonstrate at the present time His righteousness, that He might be just and the justifier of the one who has faith in Jesus." Propitiation has to do with the satisfaction of God's righteous demands. (See I John 2:2; 4:10.) The shedding of Jesus' blood fully and completely satisfies the demand of God for judgment upon sin. The blood of Jesus was of infinite value because He was not only a man but also God. (See Acts 20:28.) If He had been only a man (or if deity withdrew from Him while He continued to live on the cross), His blood could perhaps have atoned for one other person, since He was sinless. But since He was fully God, we can place no finite value on His blood. The value of His blood far exceeds all the sins that humans ever have or ever will commit.

The Old Testament uses various Hebrew words to describe the sin offerings under the law. In Isaiah 53:10, "When You make His soul an offering for sin," the word for "offering" describes an offering that exceeds the demands of justice.

The means of attaining the satisfaction with God available by the blood of Jesus is through faith. This principle contrasts with the works system of the law of Moses. This point is critical to understanding how people were saved under the old covenant, for they could not be justified by doing the works of the law of Moses. The phrase "because in His forbearance God had passed over the sins that were previously committed" explains how God forgave sins during the old covenant. He extended His forgiveness during the law of Moses to those who approached Him by faith. This He did in anticipation of the atonement that the death of Jesus would provide. The words "set forth" and "demonstrate" contrast the public death of Jesus with the hidden rituals associated with the mercy seat in the Holy of Holies in Israel's Tabernacle and Temple.

Though ancient Israel under the law of Moses could not know Jesus Christ directly, and thus could not place their faith directly in Him, they could have faith in God, and they could participate in the rituals that were symbolic of the coming Christ. (See Colossians 2:16-17; Hebrews 10:1.) If they did this, God forgave them their sins just as He today forgives those who place their faith in Jesus Christ. The Cross was God's plan for redemption from eternity (Revelation 13:8). Thus it does not matter whether we look back on the Cross in faith, or whether ancient Israel looked ahead to it in faith. (See Isaiah 53.) The benefits of the Cross are appropriated by faith, without regard to the time frame in which one happens to live.

Just as Romans 3:25 addresses the righteousness of

God in forgiving sins prior to the Cross, so Romans 3:26 addresses His righteousness in forgiving sins after the Cross. God Himself is just; no one can fault Him for His response to sin. No one who has refused His provision for redemption can legitimately complain about the consequences of sin, and no one who understands the infinite value of the blood of Jesus can fault God for forgiving sins in anticipation of the Cross or in view of the Atonement as history.

Not only is God just, He is also the One who justifies the person who places his faith (trust or reliance) in Jesus. Since it is God who justifies, no one can lodge a legitimate charge against those who have placed their faith in Jesus. (See Romans 8:33-34.)

To have faith in Jesus is not merely to assent mentally to the historical facts about His life. It is to trust in or rely upon Him to the exclusion of all else, with the understanding that genuine trust or reliance results in specific behavioral consequences. In other words, those who truly believe the gospel will obey the gospel. (See II Thessalonians 1:8.)

Justification by Faith

After demonstrating the inadequacy of the law for justification, Scripture states, "Therefore we conclude that a man is justified by faith apart from the deeds of the law" (Romans 3:28). The conclusion of the preceding discussion is that justification comes by faith *apart from* the deeds of the law. This again demonstrates the radical difference between the two covenants. There is no hint here that the new covenant is merely a continuation, revision, or updating of the old covenant. The justification that comes by faith is *apart from* the law of Moses. On the basis of one's faith exclusively in Jesus Christ, he will be counted as right in the eyes of God, for the righteousness of Jesus Christ will be reckoned to his account.

One God: One Means of Justification

Whether one is a Jew or Gentile, justification comes through faith. "There is one God who will justify the circumcised by faith and the uncircumcised through faith" (Romans 3:30). This statement would have startled Paul's Jewish readers. (See Romans 2:26-27.) Whether a person is Jewish (circumcised) or Gentile (uncircumcised), justification comes only through faith, specifically faith in Jesus Christ and in the atonement His blood provides.

There is one God (*heis ho theos*), and He relates to both Jews and Gentiles through faith. The radical monotheism of the Jews must become the radical monotheism of the Gentiles. The faith of the ancient Jews was uncompromisingly monotheistic, and there is no hint in Scripture that the faith of the church expanded to embrace some concept of plurality within God. Gentile believers can recite the ancient Shema just as legitimately as Jews. (See Deuteronomy 6:4.)

Abraham and Righteousness

A system of works lends itself to human boasting. (See Romans 3:27.) But even Abraham, the father of the Jews, could not boast before God, for his justification was by faith and not works. "For if Abraham was justified by works, he has something of which to boast, but not before God" (Romans 4:2).

If anyone has ever been saved by his own efforts, he

can boast in his achievements. But, of course, no one ever has been or can be saved on his own merits, so no one has the right to boast. Salvation is a free gift; thus we can boast only of the One who gave us the gift, not of anything we have done to deserve it.

The statement "but not before God" indicates that God knows full well His salvation is a free gift and that no one is justified in boasting. Ill-informed people may boast before one another, but they will not boast before God.

"For what does the Scripture say? 'Abraham believed God, and it was accounted to him for righteousness'" (Romans 4:3). This verse quotes Genesis 15:6. The reference from the Hebrew Scriptures proves unquestionably that Abraham was justified, not by his works, but by his faith in God. He believed what God said to be true. At this point, Abraham had done no works, yet he was accounted righteous. Abraham was not justified by the works of the law, for Abraham lived four centuries before the law of Moses was given. (See Galatians 3:17.)

Some may think that Romans at this point disputes the claim in James that Abraham was justified by works (James 2:21-23). But the problem is merely one of perception. The "faith" of which Paul wrote is a genuine trust in God that results in obedience to God's commands; the "faith" of James's letter is at best mental assent with no evidence of genuineness. In Paul's vocabulary, "works" have to do with activity intended to gain favor with God; James's use of "works" has to do with the natural consequence of genuinely held belief. There is no thought in James's letter that the works resulting from faith somehow enhance one's standing with God. They are simply the logical actions of one who is already in good standing with God.

Paul and James discussed two different events in the life of Abraham. Paul had in mind Abraham's initial response of complete, trusting belief that God's Word was true when He said, "'Look now toward heaven, and count the stars if you are able to number them. . . . So shall your descendants be'" (Genesis 15:5). Abraham "believed in the LORD, and He accounted it to him for righteousness" (Genesis 15:6). At this point, Abraham did nothing; indeed, there was nothing he could do. God had simply made a promise; Abraham genuinely believed it. Since it was genuine faith, it was accounted to Abraham for righteousness, even though it was impossible at that moment to demonstrate the genuineness of his faith in a tangible way.

Justification and Righteousness

In Paul's writings, "justification" is a legal term describing the declaration God makes concerning those who have faith in Him. The words "justify" and "righteousness" are closely related. "Justify" is from the Greek *dikaioo*; "righteousness" is from *dikaiosune*. The basic idea behind both words is the right standing one gains with God on the basis of faith in the atoning work of Christ. (See Romans 3:24-25, 28-31; 4:5; 5:1, 9; 8:1, 31-34; II Corinthians 5:21; Galatians 2:16; 3:8, 24; Titus 3:4-5.)

Romans 4:5 declares, "But to him who does not work but believes on Him who justifies the ungodly, his faith is accounted for righteousness." If a person is under the new covenant, he receives justification not by his own achievements, but by faith. This statement does not mean that in the new covenant a person with genuine faith does no work; it means that in the new covenant a person does not rely on his works for justification.

The faith required in the new covenant is not just a generic faith, but specific faith in the One who justifies the ungodly, and that is God.

God justifies the *ungodly*. In other words, God does not wait until a person demonstrates his worthiness or godliness to justify that person. Instead, He observes the faith of the ungodly person and on that basis places the righteousness of Christ to his account.

David and Righteousness

In addition to Abraham, Romans appeals to another example that Jewish readers could not deny: David. "Just as David also describes the blessedness of the man to whom God imputes righteousness apart from works: 'Blessed are those whose lawless deeds are forgiven, and whose sins are covered; blessed is the man to whom the Lord shall not impute sin'" (Romans 4:6-8). King David described the blessed condition of the person to whom God *imputes* (not "imparts") righteousness *apart from* works. (See Romans 3:21, 28.) Romans quotes a portion of Psalm 32:1-2 as an example of sins being forgiven apart from the works of the law.

From a Jewish perspective, the startling thing about this is that David lived and wrote during the old covenant. Some of the Jewish readers of Romans may have rejected the example of Abraham because Abraham lived and died long before the law was given. But David was born after the law was already in place, and it was still in effect when he died. Even so, David recognized that the imputation of righteousness was based, not on the deeds of the law, but on faith in God.

33

Imputation or Impartation?

God *imputes* righteousness; He does not *impart* it instantaneously. There is a significant difference here. To impute means to reckon, count, or credit the righteousness of Christ to the person of faith. At that moment there is not a total transformation in the nature of the person to whom righteousness is thus imputed; indeed, he still retains the sin nature. (See Galatians 5:17; I John 1:8.) If the righteousness of Christ were immediately *imparted* to believers at the new birth, it would mean the complete eradication of the sin nature.

We further see the marvel of justification by faith in that Romans uses the same word "impute" to declare that the Lord will *not* impute sin to the person of faith. The sins committed by a person of faith (if he deals with them according to I John 1:9) are not reckoned to his account. Indeed, they cannot be, for the same sin cannot be reckoned to the account of more than one person, and our sins have been imputed to Jesus, just as His righteousness is imputed to us! (See II Corinthians 5:21; Isaiah 53:4-5, 11-12.) This does not mean that on the cross Jesus became a *sinner*, any more than we become inherently righteous. It simply means that by virtue of this "great exchange," our sins were placed on Jesus' account (and He paid the penalty for them in full), and His righteousness was placed on our account.

The Termination of Ethnic Divisions

"Does this blessedness then come upon the circumcised only, or upon the uncircumcised also? For we say that faith was accounted to Abraham for righteousness" (Romans 4:9). Here Romans inquires as to whether the privilege of justification by faith is available only to the Jews (circumcised) or to the Gentiles (uncircumcised) also. The book proceeds to destroy the significance of ethnic division between the Jews and Gentiles in the new covenant. What it asserts was revolutionary to First-century Jewish readers; they came from a tradition of centuries of believing in the superiority of the Jewish people over the Gentiles due to their status as the chosen people and as the recipients of special revelation. But point by point, Romans systematically establishes that this old distinction is no longer in effect.

Righteousness before Circumcision

Romans turns again to the example of Abraham to demonstrate—no doubt to the great surprise of first-century Jewish readers—that Abraham was the father of Gentile believers before he was ever the father of Jewish believers.

Concerning the righteousness accounted to Abraham, Romans 4:10 asks, "How then was it accounted? While he was circumcised, or uncircumcised? Not while circumcised, but while uncircumcised." God did not grant righteousness to Abraham on the basis of his works. As already declared, Abraham was accounted righteous on the basis of faith. (See Romans 4:3.)

"And he received the sign of circumcision, a seal of the righteousness of the faith which he had while still uncircumcised, that he might be the father of all those who believe, though they are uncircumcised, that righteousness might be imputed to them also" (Romans 4:11). If Abraham was accounted righteous prior to being circumcised, what then was the point of circumcision? Romans here puts works in precisely the right perspective; its doctrine agrees exactly with James's emphasis on works as demonstrating the legitimacy of one's faith. Circumcision was a *sign* given to Abraham to document the genuineness of the faith he already possessed. Since Abraham's faith in God was genuine, he did not hesitate to obey God when He later commanded circumcision, or still later when He asked Abraham to offer up his only son. (See James 2:21-23.) Genuine faith always produces continuing obedience. But it is possible to have an external show of obedience that does not spring from faith.

Abraham: The Father of All Who Believe

The next statement, like many before it, was no doubt shocking to first-century Jewish readers. The reason God reckoned Abraham righteous prior to circumcision was so that Abraham could be the "father of all those who believe," including Gentiles, so that even though they are uncircumcised, they too can have righteousness imputed to them on the basis of faith. Romans 4:22 reiterates that righteousness was accounted (NKJV) or imputed to Abraham on the basis of his faith.

The Guarantee of Our Justification

Jesus "was delivered up because of our offenses, and was raised because of our justification" (Romans 4:25). Jesus was delivered up to the cross "because of" (Greek, *dia*) our offenses; He was resurrected "because of" (*dia*) our justification. It may sound strange at first to think that Jesus was raised "because of" our justification. But the point is that the resurrection of Jesus Christ proves our sins have been decisively and finally dealt with in the death and burial of Jesus, and because we are thus justified on the basis of His death, He can be resurrected with the sin problem behind Him once and for all. (See Romans 6:9-10; Hebrews 10:12, 14, 18.)

Peace: The Result of Justification

The believer's justification results in peace with God: "Therefore, having been justified by faith, we have peace with God through our Lord Jesus Christ" (Romans 5:1). The examples of Abraham and David offer conclusive proof that justification is not by works, not even by the works of the law of Moses, a God-given covenant, but by faith. In our case, justification has already occurred for all believers (Paul included himself in the first person plural pronoun "we") on the basis of faith in Jesus Christ.

The assertion that "we have peace with God" speaks of the consequence of justification. The reference is not so much to emotional peace, although that certainly follows a knowledge of the truth about one's standing with God, but to the removal of enmity between God and humans when the latter place their faith in Jesus Christ. To be justified, or to be counted right with God, by definition means to have peace with God.

A textual variant at this point reads, "Let us have peace with God." This depends upon whether one vowel is long or short. If the "o" in *echomen* is a short *omicron*, the translation is, "We have." If it is a long *omega*, the translation is, "Let us have." Since the vast majority of Greek manuscripts at this point say "We have," and since justification produces peace, it seems better to stay with the reading of the KJV and NKJV.

The peace we have with God comes "through our Lord Jesus Christ." The peace is made possible by Him, for the Atonement made justification possible. (See comments on 4:25.) Jesus, as the incarnation of God, is the one mediator between God and men. (See I Timothy 2:5.)

Jesus' Blood and Justification

"Much more then, having now been justified by His blood, we shall be saved from wrath through Him" (Romans 5:9). The justification already granted on the basis of Christ's blood provides full assurance that believers will also be saved from wrath through Jesus. God would not justify a person, then abandon him. The phrase "much more then" emphasizes the absolute certainty of the salvation from wrath that all who are justified will experience. (See I Thessalonians 5:9.)

The wrath in view here is the judicial wrath of God that He will pronounce upon all unbelievers at the final judgment. But the implication is that those who are justified will be spared any expression of the wrath of God. This would include the divine wrath visited upon the world during the Great Tribulation. The hope of believers should strengthen and mature as they contemplate the inseparable bond between justification and salvation.

Adam and Christ

Romans 5:12-21 compares the universal effects of Adam's sin and Christ's righteousness. This section of the letter explains in a carefully worded argument the negative universal impact of Adam's sin. Then it contrasts the positive universal impact of Christ's righteousness. As pervasive and destructive as Adam's sin was, the atonement provided by Christ far supersedes it, going even beyond what was necessary to reverse the effect of Adam's sin.

Romans 5:16 declares: "And the gift is not like that which came through the one who sinned. For the judgment which came from one offense resulted in condemnation, but the free gift which came from many offenses resulted in justification." The effect of Adam's sin contrasts with the gift of grace offered by Jesus Christ. The result of Adam's sin was condemnation and spiritual death; the result of the free gift offered by Jesus is justification (right standing with God) and the spiritual life. Whereas the one sin of Adam resulted in universal death, the free gift of Jesus gathered up "many offenses" (all the sins ever committed by the human race) and made atonement for them.

"For if by the one man's offense death reigned through the one, much more those who receive abundance of grace and of the gift of righteousness will reign in life through the One, Jesus Christ" (Romans 5:17). As a result of Adam's sin, death (spiritual separation from God) reigned universally. But Romans does not say that, as a consequence of Christ's work on the cross, life (spiritual fellowship with God) now reigns universally. Instead, it declares that those who will "reign in life" are those who "receive abundance of grace and of the gift of righteousness." We must receive spiritual life, and the way to do so is by faith in Jesus Christ. (See John 1:12; Romans 3:22, 26, 30; 4:11-12, 16, 24; 5:1-2.)

Romans identifies righteousness (right standing with God) as a free gift extended to those who "receive abundance of grace." The letter emphasizes that one does not earn favor with God by one's performance but receives it as a free gift by relying exclusively on Jesus Christ for salvation.

The substitutionary death of Christ on the cross was a righteous act: "Therefore, as through one man's offense judgment came to all men, resulting in condemnation, even so through one Man's righteous act the free gift came to all men, resulting in justification of life" (Romans 5:18). The parenthetical statement beginning in Romans 5:13 concludes in Romans 5:17, and now the letter contrasts the universal impact of Adam's sin directly with the universal impact of "one Man's righteous act."

The sin of Adam resulted in all people being condemned, for all participated with him in his sin, either by representation or by being present in his loins. (See Romans 5:12.) But though the righteous act of Jesus Christ results in all people being *potentially* justified, they must *receive* the free gift by faith in order to be actually justified. (See Romans 5:15.) The reason for this difference is that all people were not participants in the Atonement in the same way all were participants in Adam's sin. Although Jesus stood in complete solidarity with the human race by virtue of His genuine humanity, by the miracle of the virgin birth He was spared the sinful nature and spiritual separation from God that resulted from Adam's sin. Since God was His Father, He was not born in a state of spiritual separation from God. Thus Jesus could *represent* us on the cross, but we were not physically present in His righteous deed as we were in Adam's sin.

As a result, we participate in Adam's sin by nature, but not in Christ's atonement. In order to participate in the results of Christ's atonement, we must completely and exclusively trust in and rely upon the efficacy of the blood of Jesus for our salvation. (See Romans 3:25.) The free gift does come to all people, but it is still necessary for all to receive it.

Romans 5:19 continues the contrast between the effects of Adam and Christ on the human race: "For as by one man's disobedience many were made sinners, so also by one Man's obedience many will be made righteous." As a result of Adam's sin, the many (the entire human race[16]) became sinners. The spiritual separation from God resulting from Adam's sin assured that each human being would commit his own personal sins.

It is important to note that the human race did not initially become sinners on the basis of their individual sins; they became sinners on the basis of one man's sin. By contrast, the many (potentially the entire human race, but specifically those who receive the gift, Romans 5:17) will return to right standing with God not on the basis of their personal righteous performance, but on the basis of "one Man's obedience."

This point is in perfect harmony with the emphasis throughout this letter that people gain right standing with God not on the basis of their righteous deeds, but on the basis of the righteousness of Jesus Christ. Just as we experience spiritual separation from God as a consequence not of specific sins we have committed, but of what Adam did, so we experience spiritual reconciliation with God not by our own righteous works, but by the work of Jesus Christ. This truth can remove forever the fear that our right standing with God depends upon our own performance. Those who are secure in their right standing with God find it much easier to conform to right behavior than those who live constantly in the fear that they must "get good to get God." (See Romans 7:5-11.)

41

In the same context, we find, "So that as sin reigned in death, even so grace might reign through righteousness to eternal life through Jesus Christ our Lord" (Romans 5:21). Just as sin universally condemned all people to spiritual separation from God (death), so grace provides universal right standing with God, which will result in eternal life for all who receive it. (See Romans 5:15.) This eternal life is through Jesus Christ our Lord.

The Practical Effects of Righteousness

In a discussion of the practical effects of the gift of righteousness, Romans 6:13 says, "And do not present your members as instruments of unrighteousness to sin, but present yourselves to God as being alive from the dead, and your members as instruments of righteousness to God." We are not to lend our "members" for sinful purposes, but to allow them to be used for right purposes. The "members" are any part of a human being's resources over which he has control. This word certainly includes any member of his physical body, but it also includes his mind and aspects of his immaterial being. We are to present our members to God on the basis of the spiritual life that sprang from identification with Jesus in His death.

On the same theme, Romans 6:16 continues, "Do you not know that to whom you present yourselves slaves to obey, you are that one's slaves whom you obey, whether of sin to death, or of obedience to righteousness?" If believers yield themselves to obey the leading of the Holy Spirit to do what is right, they become "slaves" of right living. "And having been set free from sin, you became slaves of righteousness" (Romans 6:18). Not only are believers set free from sin's control, they also—by virtue of their union with Christ—become "slaves of righteousness." This does not mean they become robots or automatons with no choices of their own, but that they no longer owe allegiance to sin. Their loyalties now belong to what is right.

There is a connection between righteousness and holiness. "Present your members as slaves of righteousness for holiness" (Romans 6:19). When a believer surrenders his members in service of right living, holiness results. The production of holiness is the goal of the process of sanctification. By definition, holiness is identification with the character of God in His moral perfections.

"For when you were slaves of sin, you were free in regard to righteousness" (Romans 6:20). Before a person becomes a believer, when he is still a slave to the sin nature, he is completely free from right living. This does not mean he is as wicked or perverse as he could possibly be, but it does mean that apart from union with Christ there is nothing right. (See Romans 3:10-18.) Sin mars the total realm of human existence, materially and immaterially. An unregenerate person may be relatively moral, but morality is not righteousness in the eyes of God. Only by identifying with Jesus Christ in His death, burial, and resurrection can one find genuine righteousness.

The Atonement makes it possible "that the righteous requirement of the law might be fulfilled in us who do not walk according to the flesh but according to the Spirit" (Romans 8:4). Through the Atonement, Jesus accomplished what the law could never do: He provided a way for people to come into right relationship with God.

It would be a mistake to think that "the righteous

requirement of the law" means that we are under obligation to fulfill the law of Moses. The law of Moses was temporary, and it terminated with the coming of the Messiah. (See Romans 7:4; 10:4; Galatians 3:23-25; Hebrews 10:9.) Romans does not say here "that the *law* might be fulfilled *by* us," but "that the righteous *requirement* of the law might be fulfilled *in* us."[17]

Grammatically, the latter half of this verse does not mean that the righteous requirement of the law is fulfilled in us *as long as* or *provided* we walk in the Spirit and not according to the flesh. It means that believers no longer walk according to the flesh; their source of life is the Spirit, although they do not always allow themselves to be perfectly led by the Spirit.

Since Christ dwells in the believer, "the body is dead because of sin, but the Spirit is life because of righteousness" (Romans 8:10). Contextually, the word "body" refers to the human body (Romans 8:11). Even though the human body—even of a believer—is subject to death because of the lingering effects of the sin nature, the believer still possesses eternal life through the indwelling Spirit. The Spirit imparts life to the believer because the righteousness of Jesus Christ is imputed to him. Death will be the final effect of sin that is destroyed in the believer's life by the resurrection. (See I Corinthians 15:54-57.)

The First Step in Conforming to the Image of Jesus Christ

All things work together for good to those who love God and who are the called according to His purpose (Romans 8:28). This process works as follows: "For whom He foreknew, He also predestined to be conformed to the image of His Son, that He might be the firstborn among many brethren. Moreover whom He predestined, these He also called; whom He called, these He also justified; and whom He justified, these He also glorified" (Romans 8:29-30). A series of verbs leads up to the final goal of glorification. They begin with God's foreknowledge, proceed to predestination, then to calling, then to justification, and finally to glorification.

It is essential to note that the process begins with the foreknowledge of God, not with predestination. Although it is impossible for us to comprehend the foreknowledge of God since we have no foreknowledge (Proverbs 27:1; James 4:14), the Scripture declares that God is omniscient. He knows all things. (See Psalm 139:1-6; Isaiah 46:10; 48:5; 57:15; Jeremiah 1:5; 23:24; Romans 11:2; I Peter 1:2.) Since God knows all things—past, present, and future—He knows who will come to Him. But this does not mean God has predestined some to be saved and others to be lost. God's foreknowledge of the choices people will make is not at all the same thing as God making their decisions for them. Although God knows who will be saved or lost, He still leaves the choice up to the individual, and it is a free choice. (See John 3:16; Revelation 22:17; Acts 17:30; II Peter 3:9.)

Those whom God foreknows will come to Him, He has "predestined to be conformed to the image of His Son." This is the purpose of God mentioned in Romans 8:28. Conformity to the image of God's Son comes by the process of sanctification. As believers go through all of life's experiences with their love for God intact, they gradually conform more and more to the image of Christ;

they are shaped to reflect His character more accurately.

The ultimate expression of this process will occur at the "revealing of the sons of God" (Romans 8:19). At that point, believers will fully and completely reflect Christ's image. This will happen on the basis of the believer's identification with Christ, not only in His death and burial but also in His resurrection. (See Romans 6:2-8.) Thus Jesus is "the firstborn among many brethren." His resurrection from the dead presages the similar resurrection of many. (See I Corinthians 15:20, 51-58.)

When we let the context define the calling of Romans 8:30, we avoid confusion as to whether God predestines individuals to be saved or lost. The call to salvation is universal; all are called to repent of their sins and come to Christ. But contextually, the call of this verse is the call to be conformed to the image of Jesus Christ (verses 28-29). This call extends only to those who have previously responded to the universal call to salvation. God predestines to be conformed to the image of His Son those who first respond to His call to salvation.

The first step in being conformed to the image of Jesus Christ is justification. The final step in being conformed to the image of Jesus Christ is glorification. (See Romans 8:18, 21, 23.) We see the certainty of God's intention to bring believers into full conformity with the image of His Son by the description of the believer's glorification as having already occurred. As far as God is concerned, the glorification of the believer is an accomplished fact. He completes every good work He begins (Philippians 1:6), so the only thing that would thwart God's intention is if the believer himself turns away from his love for God and thus from his call to be conformed to Christ's image.

It Is God Who Justifies

In a rhetorical question, Paul asked, "Who shall bring a charge against God's elect? It is God who justifies" (Romans 8:33). No one can legitimately bring a charge against the elect of God. This does not imply that the elect are sinless, but that the righteousness of Jesus Christ has been imputed to them. Since believers are God's elect, and since God has dealt permanently with the sin problem on the cross of Calvary, and since believers have been united with Jesus Christ in His death, burial and resurrection, no accuser—including Satan (Revelation 12:10)—can find any legal basis for making a charge against them.

Israel's Present Rejection

In view of God's sovereign election of the nation of Israel as discussed in Romans 9:1-29, it would seem reasonable to ask why the nation was not enjoying the favor of God at the time of the writing of this letter. The next section of the letter (Romans 9:30-10:21) is a response to that question. The reason national Israel was experiencing God's rejection is that they had rejected the Messiah, Jesus Christ.

"What shall we say then? That Gentiles, who did not pursue righteousness, have attained to righteousness, even the righteousness of faith" (Romans 9:30). We see the universal nature of God's mercy in that even the Gentiles, who had no written revelation (Romans 1:19-20), and who thus made no effort to pursue righteousness, were nevertheless recipients of God's mercy. Since they responded to His mercy in faith, they attained to the righteousness (right standing with God) that springs from faith.

47

"But Israel, pursuing the law of righteousness, has not attained to the law of righteousness. Why? Because they did not seek it by faith, but as it were by the works of the law. For they stumbled at that stumbling stone" (Romans 9:31-32). Israel received revelation superior to the Gentiles and pursued righteousness on the basis of the law of Moses. They did not, however, attain right standing with God, because they sought righteousness on the basis of works and not faith.[18] (See Hebrews 4:2.) The stone at which Israel stumbled was Jesus Christ and the atonement He provided. (See I Peter 2:4-8.)

Continuing this theme, Romans 10:3 says of Israel, "For they being ignorant of God's righteousness, and seeking to establish their own righteousness, have not submitted to the righteousness of God." National Israel was ignorant of the righteousness God promised to provide, and had now provided, in the Atonement. Instead of accepting the work of Christ on the cross as the satisfaction of God's righteous judgment on their sins (I John 2:2), the nation of Israel sought to establish their own righteousness on the basis of their works. Most of the first-century Jews simply could not believe that the death of one man on a cross could do for them what they and their ancestors had spent their lifetimes trying to do by diligent and exacting obedience to the works of the law.

Christ: The End of the Law

But "Christ is the end of the law for righteousness to everyone who believes" (Romans 10:4). Jesus Christ is the conclusion of the law of Moses. He was the ultimate goal toward which the law pointed (Galatians 3:24), and He fulfilled every prophetic element of the law (Matthew

5:17; Luke 24:44; John 5:39). After the coming of Christ, the law was obsolete. (See Romans 7:4; Hebrews 10:9.)

Not only did Christ end the law, His substitutionary death on the cross provides right standing with God ("righteousness") for all who place their trust exclusively in Him for salvation. By definition, this means a person must turn away from attempting to attain right standing with God on the basis of the law (Romans 9:31-32) or any similar works-oriented system. It is impossible to be "married" to Christ and thus to participate in the benefits of the new covenant established by Him and at the same time relate to God on the basis of the law of Moses or any other system.

God intended for the entire sacrificial system of the law of Moses to point national Israel to the ultimate sacrifice that would take away the sin of the world. (See John 1:29.) The blood of the sacrificial animals never resulted in the removal of any sins; God did not intended for it to. (See Hebrews 10:1-4; Galatians 2:16.) All that the sacrifice of animals accomplished, and all God intended it to accomplish, was to function as a "shadow" of the supreme sacrifice that would deal with the sin problem. (See Hebrews 10:1; Colossians 2:16-17; John 1:29; I Corinthians 5:7; Revelation 13:8.)

The only Israelites for whom the sacrificial system was of any salvific value were those who offered the sacrifices with faith toward God in anticipation of the ultimate sacrifice, however vague their understanding of that ultimate sacrifice may have been. (See Hebrews 11:6, 39-40; Isaiah 52:13-15; 53:1-12.) Even then, it was not the blood of the sacrificial animal that atoned for sin, but the blood of Jesus Christ, which was merely represented by

49

the blood shed under the law of Moses.

It may seem strange to think that the blood of Jesus Christ could atone for sins before the Messiah actually came into the world and thus before He died on the cross, but this was possible because He was the "Lamb slain from the foundation of the world" (Revelation 13:8). Since God, who "calls those things which do not exist as though they did" (Romans 4:17), knew people would sin even before He created them, from the beginning He determined to provide for their redemption by the Incarnation and Atonement. Since this was a settled fact in the mind of God, He was able to deal with the sin problem on the basis of the blood of Jesus prior to the Cross just as surely as He is able to deal with it now after the Cross.

In every age, salvation has been available only through faith in God on the basis of the provision He made (or would make, if one lived prior to the Cross) by the blood of Jesus. The only difference between the ages is in the content of faith (the level of revelation) and the expression of faith (for Noah, it was building a boat; for Abraham, it was leaving Ur; for Israel after Sinai, it was the law of Moses; for the church, it is the new birth).

The Righteousness of the Law

"For Moses writes about the righteousness which is of the law, 'The man who does those things shall live by them'" (Romans 10:5). The only righteousness available exclusively through the law of Moses was the temporal, earth-bound, nonsalvific righteousness that came from the works of the law. It was not the right standing with God that comes from faith; it was the right standing gained in the human community of national Israel as one adhered to the demands of the law. (See Leviticus 18:5; Galatians 3:12.) The "life" promised those who embraced the works of the law was not eternal life, but long life in the land promised to Israel's father, Abraham.

An examination of the "second law," Deuteronomy, points this out. The significant themes found in the "second law" include "life," "righteousness," and "law/covenant." The first two of these topics have to do not with eternal life or moral righteousness, but with temporal life in the Promised Land and external right-eousness related to obedience to the commandments of the law/covenant.

There is no reference to eternal life in the Book of Deuteronomy. Instead, the "life" in view is connected with "length of days" or "prolonging of days" *in the land.* (See Deuteronomy 6:2; 30:20; 32:47.) It speaks of life in rela-tion to the temporal blessings resulting from obedience to the law, as opposed to death relating to the temporal curs-ings resulting from disobedience. (See Deuteronomy 30:19.) It equates life with good, death with evil. (See Deuteronomy 30:15). The good (life) has to do with the blessings of long life in the land; evil (death) has to do with the curses that would result from disobedience, all of which were temporal. (See Deuteronomy 30:16-20.) If the people were not obedient to the law, their life would "hang in doubt"; they would have no assurance of life. (See Deuteronomy 28:66.)

The righteousness described in Deuteronomy is dependent upon obedience to the law. It is not an imputed righteousness as seen in the new covenant, and it is cer-tainly not an inherent, internal moral righteousness.

Under the terms of the law, one could be righteous

through exclusively external behavior: "And it shall be our righteousness, if we observe to do all these commandments before the LORD our God, as he hath commanded us" (Deuteronomy 6:25, KJV). A person could attain this kind of righteousness by a work such as returning to a man before sundown the cloak he had offered as collateral for a loan (Deuteronomy 24:13). The sacrifices required by the law were "sacrifices of righteousness" (Deuteronomy 33:19). They did not reflect or guarantee purity of heart; they merely measured Israel's external conformity to the conditions of the covenant. Israel did not enter the land because of inherent moral righteousness (Deuteronomy 9:4-5). They entered in spite of the fact that they were "stiffnecked" (Deuteronomy 9:6). Yet these "stiffnecked" people could be called "righteous" in terms of the law.

Deuteronomy equates the terms "law" and "covenant." The covenant was a law covenant, that is, it was a conditional covenant depending upon obedience to its requirements. (See Deuteronomy 4:13, 44; 5:2; 9:9, 11.) The central requirement of the covenant was adherence to the Ten Commandments, eight of which were negative. Disobedience to any of these commandments was a violation of the covenant. (See Deuteronomy 4:23.) The curses written in the "book of the law" are called "the curses of the covenant" (Deuteronomy 29:21).

The covenant was bilateral: it depended both upon the faithfulness of God and the obedience of Israel. God could, of course, be counted on to keep His promises. (See Deuteronomy 4:31.) But He would keep the positive provisions of the covenant only if Israel was obedient to its terms. (See Deuteronomy 7:12.)

After the covenant made at Sinai, the Lord made further and quite graphic statements concerning the positive results of keeping the covenant and the negative consequences of disobedience. (See Deuteronomy 29:1, 9, 12, 14, 21, 25). All of these results, positive or negative, related to the quality of Israel's life in the land.

When Moses finished writing the law, he placed it in the *ark of the covenant* (Deuteronomy 31:9, 24, 26), so called because it was the centerpiece of the covenant God made with Israel. It is significant that the tables of the *law* were to be deposited in the ark of the *covenant*. The two ideas of law and covenant were inseparably bound together.

God never intended for the law given to Israel at Sinai to provide a means of eternal salvation or life. It was a temporal covenant given exclusively to Israel to govern their life in the land promised to their forefather Abraham. Obedience to the terms of this covenant provided them with a "law/covenant righteousness," or an external righteousness. The covenant was conditional: its blessings depended upon Israel's faithfulness to its terms. Failure to adhere consistently to the commandments contained in the law would result in specific curses and eventual expulsion from the land.

The righteousness available on the basis of adherence to the law of Moses was so irrevocably tied to one's works that Paul described it as "my own righteousness" and contrasted it with the "righteousness which is from God by faith" (Philippians 3:9).

The Righteousness of Faith

Romans contrasts the righteousness of faith with the righteousness of works under the law: "But the righteousness of faith speaks in this way, 'Do not say in your heart, "Who will ascend into heaven?"' (that is, to bring Christ down from above) or, '"Who will descend into the abyss?"' (that is, to bring Christ up from the dead)" (Romans 10:6-7). Herein we see the radical difference between the righteousness available on the basis of the works of the law and the righteousness available as a gift from God on the basis of faith.

Romans 10 demonstrates this contrast by a free rendering of the Septuagint translation of Deuteronomy 30:11-14.[19] As A. T. Robertson points out, Paul "does not quote Moses as saying this or meaning this."[20] Since this is so, there may not be much to gain here by examining the passage in Deuteronomy from which this quotation is drawn. The Deuteronomy passage has to do with the charge given by Moses to Israel as they were preparing to enter the Promised Land. (See Deuteronomy 30:11-14.) In brief, Moses' address concerned the covenant God had established with Israel at Mount Sinai; they did not have to go somewhere to get it. It was near them, in their mouth and in their heart, so they could obey it. (See Deuteronomy 6:6-25.)

Paul's inspired use of these words takes their significance beyond the law of Moses. Thus Romans 10:5 uses them to contrast the "righteousness of faith" with the "righteousness which is of the law." The righteousness of faith does not focus on what people can do, but on what God has already done. Specifically, the righteousness of faith does not ask, "Who will ascend into heaven?" in an attempt to bring the Messiah down from above. Nor does it ask, "Who will descend into the abyss?" in an attempt to bring the Messiah up from the dead. In other words, the righteousness of faith does not attempt to force the incarnation or the resurrection of the Messiah; it recognizes them as the acts of God. God has done on our behalf what we could never do.

Instead of attempting to participate in its own salvation by claiming human merit for the incarnation or resurrection of the Messiah, the righteousness of faith declares, "The word is near you even in your mouth and in your heart." That is, the "word of faith," the good news of justification by faith, has been declared to us "which we preach." (See Romans 10:8.)

"If you confess with your mouth the Lord Jesus and believe in your heart that God has raised Him from the dead, you will be saved. For with the heart one believes to righteousness, and with the mouth confession is made to salvation" (Romans 10:9-10). The new covenant message of justification by faith is "the word (*rhema*, "saying") of faith." It promises right standing (righteousness) with God on the basis, not of works, but of faith in the Lord Jesus, which is confessed with one's mouth. In essence, the person who puts his faith (trust) exclusively in Jesus Christ and His substitutionary, atoning work for salvation will be saved. (See Romans 10:11, 13.) Faith does not, of course, preclude the necessity of obedience to the gospel, for we cannot separate saving faith from obedient response to the gospel message. (See II Thessalonians 1:8.)

The facts we must believe in order to receive the benefits of the new covenant are that Jesus is Lord (the Greek equivalent of the Hebrew *Yahweh*) and that God raised the Messiah, Jesus, from the dead. But contextually, belief in His resurrection includes the believer being united with Him in this event. (See Romans 6:4-5, 8.)

Verse 9 refers first to confession (from the Greek *homologia*, which means "to say the same thing as" or "to agree with") of the mouth and then to belief in the heart. Verse 10 reverses the order. Paul may have had in mind the psalmist's statement, "I believed, therefore I spoke" (Psalm 116:10). Obviously, confession of the mouth is of no value unless it springs from genuine faith in the heart.

What these verses do is explain the nature and result of faith: If a person believes in Jesus Christ as His Savior and Redeemer, and if he believes in the substitutionary atonement provided by the death, burial, and resurrection of Jesus Christ (which means he believes right standing with God comes on the basis of Jesus' work and not our works), and if he gives evidence of his faith by confessing (agreeing with God) that the Lord Jesus has made every provision needed for right standing with God, he will enjoy the salvific benefits of the Atonement. This truth does not, of course, denigrate the necessity of genuine repentance and of being united with Christ in His death, burial, and resurrection by means of water baptism and receiving the gift of the Holy Spirit. (See Matthew 28:19; Mark 16:16; Luke 24:47; Acts 1:5; 2:1-4, 38; 8:12-17; 10:44-48; 19:1-6; Romans 6:2-8.) But it does declare that faith is first and foremost and that only faith can produce and validate what follows, whether it is repentance, water baptism, or the receiving of the Holy Spirit.

Nothing in these verses lends support to the so-called "positive confession" or "word-of-faith" theologies. These ideas are not far removed from the metaphysical teachings of non-Christian religions or, at best, from the "positive thinking" or "positive mental attitude" systems popular among some in the self-improvement movement. They miss the point of this passage altogether and lack scriptural support. The idea that we can create our own realities or bring things into existence by adopting a specific mental attitude and by speaking things into existence is totally foreign to this passage.

Indeed, that is just the opposite of the point here. If such a thing could be, it would be the ultimate expression of works, righteousness and of self-reliance. One could then boast in what he had achieved by his own mental discipline and vocalization. Instead, Romans teaches that believers must abandon the religion of self-reliance (in this case, reliance upon the works of the law of Moses for salvation) and cast themselves without reservation upon the work Jesus Christ has done for them. Unless a person believes that he can do nothing for himself to merit or earn salvation and that Jesus Christ has done everything for him, he cannot be saved. This concept is light-years removed from the "positive confession" idea, which focuses on a person's work in mental imaging and vocalization as the basis upon which he receives the free gifts of God.

The Essence of the Kingdom of God

The next mention of righteousness is in Romans 14:17: "For the kingdom of God is not food and drink, but righteousness and peace and joy in the Holy Spirit." In a discussion about the mutual responsibilities of the strong and weak brethren to accept one another, Romans points out that the kingdom of God is not defined by issues relating to diet, but by the work of the Holy Spirit in the life of the believer: righteousness (right standing with God), peace (Romans 5:1), and joy. This list is similar to the fruit of the Spirit of Galatians 5:22-23. Since the matters of diet, and, by implication, observation of days (Romans 14:5-6), are not the defining issues, they should never be issues of fellowship. Entry is gained and maintained in the kingdom of God by the birth of the Spirit (I Corinthians 12:13), not by embracing a certain diet or calendar. (See Galatians 4:9-11.)

Notes

[1]Alister McGrath, *Justification by Faith* (Grand Rapids, MI: Zondervan Publishing House, 1988), 9.

[2]Walter Bauer, *A Greek-English Lexicon of the New Testament and Other Early Christian Literature*, trans. William F. Arndt and F. Wilbur Gingrich, revised and augmented by F. Wilbur Gingrich and Frederick W. Danker, second edition (Chicago: University of Chicago Press, 1979), 172.

[3]*Ibid.*, 198.

[4]Ladd, *Theology*, (Grand Rapids, MI: Eerdmans, 1993), 437.

[5]*Ibid.*

[6]*Ibid.*

[7]*Ibid.*, 440.

[8]*Ibid.*

[9]*Ibid.*

[10]*Ibid.*

[11]Ladd, 439.

[12]McGrath, *Justification*, 26.

[13]*Ibid.*, 27.

[14]In the Greek text of Romans 3:21, the word "law" (*nomos*) does not have the definite article, which indicates that Romans at this point is discussing the *principle* of law and not the law of Moses exclusively.

[15]Under the old covenant, people received benefits as a result of obedience to the law of Moses. (See Exodus 15:26; Deuteronomy 6:2; 11:22-23; 13:17-18; 19:9; 26:18-19; 27:26; 28:1, 15; 30:8-9; Galatians 3:10; 5:3; James 2:10.) In this sense we can call it a "covenant of works," although we do not use this term as do covenant theologians when they refer to a covenant of works God supposedly made with Adam prior to his sin in the Garden of Eden.

[16]In the Greek the definite article is present (*hoi polloi*), indicating not just "many" as in a large number, but "*the* many," as in all humanity.

[17]See discussion under "Fulfilling the Law's Righteous Requirement" in chapter 2.

[18]See discussion under "Pursue Right Standing with God by Faith" in chapter 4.

[19]This use of the Septuagint raises the question of its reliability as a translation. The Old Testament was originally written in Hebrew, with small portions in Daniel and Ezra originally written in Aramaic. The Septuagint was a Greek translation of the Hebrew Scriptures accomplished in about 250 B.C. In some cases, New Testament writers quote the Septuagint; in others, they quote the Hebrew directly; in still others, they apparently provide their own translation. The quality of translation in the Septuagint is not even; some books are more carefully translated than others.

If we keep in mind that the writers of the New Testament were inspired of God equally with the original writers of the Old Testament, it will help us understand their use of Old Testament passages. Their use of the Hebrew Scriptures was directed by the Holy Spirit. If the Holy Spirit wished to invest new meaning into the words of Old Testament prophecies, or if He wished to make use of the essence of an Old Testament prophecy and to add additional significance to it by adopting the reading of the Septuagint or any other translation (including that of the human authors of the New Testament), He was certainly free to do so. The words were His. There may be an analogy here with the way a human author can revisit words he has previously written and revise them to take on new or additional meaning. In the case of Scripture, of course, the words of the New Testament are inspired of God, and are thus without error, just as the words of the Old Testament. When the New Testament quotes the Old Testament in any form, we must interpret the New Testament statement in its context. If the New Testament quotes the Hebrew Scriptures and claims they are fulfilled in a specific New Testament event, we may gain additional insight for interpretation from examining the Old Testament context as well. But in this case the interpreter must be certain the New Testament actually claims the Hebrew Scripture is *fulfilled* in the New Testament event.

The inspiration of Scripture ended with the writing of the last book of the New Testament by the apostle John. (See Revelation 22:18-19.) For that reason, we do not have the authority today to invest new meaning into Old Testament Scriptures. No one in our day is inspired equally with the writers of the New Testament to expand on the meaning of any inspired writing. The task before today's interpreter is to seek to understand all of Scripture in its original context.

[20]A. T. Robertson, *Word Pictures in the New Testament* (Grand Rapids, MI: Baker Book House, 1931) 4:388.

Law:
Leading Israel to the Messiah

The Pauline Epistles reveal a variety of reasons for which God gave the law of Moses to Israel at Sinai.[1] But one of the clearest and most dramatic reasons is described in Galatians 3:23-25: The law of Moses was a strict disciplinarian[2] that served to guard Israel until the coming of the Messiah, Jesus Christ. With the coming of Christ, there is no longer any need for the law. "But before faith came, we were kept under guard by the law, kept for the faith which would afterward be revealed. Therefore the law was our tutor to bring us to Christ, that we might be justified by faith. But after faith has come, we are no longer under a tutor." This statement does not mean that no one was justified by faith during the law,[3] but that people's faith could not be specifically and directly in the person of Jesus Christ until His coming.

Although Romans discusses the law of Moses from a

variety of perspectives, its overriding view of the law is the same as that in Galatians: The law was a temporary covenant given exclusively to national Israel to provide structure and discipline until the coming of Messiah.

Judged by the Law

The first mention of the law of Moses in Romans is in Romans 2:12: "For as many as have sinned without law will also perish without law, and as many as have sinned in the law will be judged by the law." We see God's complete impartiality in that He will judge people strictly on the basis of the revelation they have received.

The Gentiles, who were not recipients of the law of Moses, will be judged, not by the law, but by general revelation. Since none of them live up perfectly to the standard of general revelation they have received, Gentiles will perish "without law," or without regard to the requirements of the law of Moses.

The Jews, who were recipients of special revelation by means of the written Scriptures and the law of Moses, will be judged according to the requirements of the law. Since, like the Gentiles, Jews also fail to live up to the level of revelation they have received, they will suffer the consequences of disobedience that the law describes.

Judged by Conscience

Even though the Gentiles did not have the law of Moses to define sin for them, they did have the testimony of conscience, which had at least some points in common with the law of Moses: "For when Gentiles, who do not have the law, by nature do the things contained in the law, these, although not having the law, are a law to themselves, who show the work of the law written in their hearts, their conscience also bearing witness, and between themselves their thoughts accusing or else excusing them" (Romans 2:14-15).

No Gentile's conscience would inform him of the necessity of keeping commandments like the Sabbath, annual feast days, the dietary laws, civil laws, agricultural laws, laws pertaining to the content of fabric suitable for clothing, and so forth. Commandments dealing with issues like these, and many more, were included in the law of Moses. The only point of commonality the Gentile's conscience would have with the law of Moses would be where the law touched on moral issues. When Gentiles adhere to moral codes that are in harmony with the moral commandments of the law, they give testimony that they "are a law to themselves." That is, they too are the recipients of revelation, though it is not as advanced as the revelation extended to Israel.

Romans does not imply here that any Gentile is perfectly obedient to the law of his conscience. Indeed, the summary of this entire section is the news that "all have sinned and fall short of the glory of God" (Romans 3:23). The point in these verses is not that some Gentiles will be justified by their adherence to general revelation, for none are perfectly obedient to the revelation they have received, however minimal it may be. (See Romans 3:10-12.) This section of the letter explains not how some may be saved because of their perfect conformity to revelation, but why all are lost: They all fall short of perfection. That Romans does not mean any Gentile is perfectly obedient to his conscience is seen in that the Gentile's conscience both accuses and excuses him. In other words, when the Gentile transgresses what he knows to do, his conscience accuses him. When he does what he knows to do, his conscience excuses him.

Boasting in the Law

Directly addressing Jewish readers, Romans 2:17-20 declares, "Indeed you are called a Jew, and rest on the law, and make your boast in God, and know His will, and approve the things that are excellent, being instructed out of the law, and are confident that you yourself are a guide to the blind, a light to those who are in darkness, an instructor of the foolish, a teacher of babes, having the form of knowledge and truth in the law."

Whereas some Gentile believers in Rome were apparently somewhat antagonistic toward Jewish believers, as indicated by their boasting and reveling in their freedom from the law of Moses (Romans 11:13, 18, 20, 25; 14-15), some Jews were also critical of the Gentiles, as indicated in Romans 2:17-3:2, 9; 4:1-22.

These Jews insisted on retaining their ethnic identity, and they looked to the law of Moses as reason to claim superiority over Gentile believers who had received only general revelation. An extremely rare Greek word is found in Romans 2:17, translated "rest." It is found elsewhere in Scripture only in Luke 10:6. A form of *pauo* ("stop," "cease"), it describes stopping to lean on something with the idea of being supported and held up by it. The idea in this verse is that the Jewish believers were continuing to trust in the law of Moses instead of advancing on to fully embrace the new covenant, which by definition requires releasing the old covenant. (See Hebrews 10:9.)

The Jewish believers who continued to rely on the law of Moses claimed, on the basis of the law, to know the will of God and to have priority on excellence. Their claim was in opposition to the Gentile believers who, from the Jewish perspective, could not know the will of God or approve excellent things because they did not have the law.

The arrogance of these Jews is apparent. They were confident that they were qualified to guide the "blind" (Gentiles), that they were a light to those in darkness (Gentiles), that they were able to instruct the "foolish" (Gentiles) and "babes" (Gentiles). They felt superior because they were the recipients of superior revelation. The Gentiles had only general revelation (creation and conscience); the Jews had the law, which imparted knowledge and truth.

By a series of rhetorical questions, all demanding a positive answer, Romans points out that these Jewish believers, while boasting in superior revelation, violated the very revelation in which they boasted and thus dishonored God just as did the Gentiles: "You, therefore, who teach another, do you not teach yourself? You who preach that a man should not steal, do you steal? You who say, 'Do not commit adultery,' do you commit adultery? You who abhor idols, do you rob temples? You who make your boast in the law, do you dishonor God through breaking the law?" (Romans 2:21-23).

The Law is One Unit

The law, with its 613 commandments, stands as one unit according to Romans 2:25: "For circumcision is indeed profitable if you keep the law; but if you are a breaker of the law, your circumcision has become uncircumcision." Circumcision identified Israel as the physical descendants of Abraham. (See Genesis 17:10-14.) It was also incorporated into the law of Moses. (See Exodus 4:26; Joshua 5:2; Leviticus 12:3.) There was value to circumcision for a Jew if it was accompanied by adherence to the rest of the law, but if a Jew violated any of the commandments of the law, his circumcision was of no value. He was no different than a Gentile who had never been circumcised. The boasting of Jews against the Gentiles was pointless, because they violated the law in which they boasted and thus were no different than the Gentiles.

This verse does not encourage Jewish believers to revert back to the law in their search for righteousness. Elsewhere this letter plainly states that the old covenant, and thus the law of Moses with which it was synonymous, has ended and been replaced by the new covenant with the coming of Jesus Christ. (See Romans 3:20-22, 24, 27, 28; 5:20; 7:4, 6; 8:2-3; 9:30-33; 10:3-4; 11:6, 27.) The solution for Jewish believers was not to try harder to keep the law perfectly. Instead, what they needed to do was cease judging Gentile believers and turn away from their boasting in their superior revelation. That the Jews had received a better revelation than the Gentiles did not make them better people. They were just as sinful, weak, and imperfect as their Gentile counterparts.

When Does Uncircumcision Become Circumcision?

To demonstrate that Jews are not ethnically superior to Gentiles, Romans 2:26 asks, "Therefore, if an uncircumcised man keeps the righteous requirements of the law, will not his uncircumcision be counted as circumcision?" This does not seem to be a suggestion that any Gentile actually did obey the law of Moses perfectly; the larger context of Romans 1-3 is that all people, whether Gentile or Jew, fail to measure up to the revelation they have received. (See Romans 3:23.) The point seems, rather, to be hypothetical: If a Gentile were successful in keeping the law, no Jew could claim superiority to him. The physical circumcision of the Jew would not make him a better person than the uncircumcised Gentile. This truth underscores the assertion that "there is no partiality with God" (Romans 2:11). One person is not superior to another because of any physical characteristic like circumcision.

Gentiles Judging Jews?

Next, Romans 2:27 asks, "And will not the physically uncircumcised, if he fulfills the law, judge you who, even with your written code and circumcision, are a transgressor of the law?"

No doubt it was shocking to first-century Jewish readers to hear that there was any scenario in which a Gentile could be morally superior to them. Again, Romans does not suggest that this has actually happened; all Gentiles are sinners as are all Jews (Romans 3:23). But the point of this verse, as in Romans 3:26, is that there really is no difference between the Jews and the Gentiles. That the Jews had their "written code" (the law of Moses) and "circumcision" (as evidence that they were physically descended from Abraham) did not make them inherently better people than the Gentiles.

A Broader View of "Law"

After Romans 3:10-18 quotes from a variety of Old Testament sources, Romans 3:19 says, "Now we know that whatever the law says, it says to those who are under the law, that every mouth may be stopped, and all the world may become guilty before God."

The purpose in the preceding quotes is here revealed: All the world is guilty before God; no one can legitimately open his mouth to accuse God of being unjust in proclaiming judgment against him. (See Romans 3:4.)

The use of the word "law" here is instructive. The quotes come from "the law" yet they are from Psalms and Isaiah. This example illustrates that the word "law" is used in a variety of ways. Sometimes it refers to the entire Old Testament (Matthew 5:17-18; Romans 3:10-19; Isaiah 28:11 with I Corinthians 14:21; John 5:10 with Jeremiah 17:21); sometimes to the Pentateuch (Luke 24:44; I Corinthians 14:34 with Genesis 3:16; I Chronicles 16:40); sometimes to the Book of Deuteronomy (Deuteronomy 1:1-5; 27:1-8; Joshua 8:30-35); sometimes to the Ten Commandments (Exodus 20:1-17; 24:12); sometimes to a specific regulation within the law of Moses (Leviticus 7:7); and sometimes to a human manner or custom (II Samuel 7:19, where the Hebrew *torah* is translated "manner"). In the New Testament the Greek *nomos* ("law") is used in reference also to the law of faith (Romans 3:27), the law of the mind and the law of sin (Romans 7:23), and the law of the Spirit of life (Romans 8:2). The phrase "sin is the transgression of the law" in I John 3:4 means "sin is lawlessness." This is the broadest use of the word "law." That is, sin is "defection from any of God's standards."[4] As with any other word, we must seek the definition of the word "law" from its context.

The quotations from the Hebrew Scriptures demonstrate the sinfulness of the Jews from the very revelation they treasured and because of which they claimed superiority over the Gentiles. The Jews were "under the law" (bound to obedience to the Hebrew Scriptures), and because their own Scriptures declared the universal sinfulness of humanity, including Jews, there could be no question that "all the world" (by implication, Jews as well as Gentiles) was "guilty before God."

No Justification by the Law

Reiterating a theme declared elsewhere, Romans 3:20 indicates the hopelessness of Jewish boasting in the law: "Therefore by the deeds of the law no flesh will be justified in His sight, for by the law is the knowledge of sin." (See also Acts 13:39; Galatians 2:16; 3:21; Romans 3:28; 4:5.) No one can be justified by the deeds of the law, because that is not the purpose for which the law of Moses was given. Its purpose was not to provide a means of salvific justification; among its purposes was to define sin. (See Romans 7:7.) The law did not create sin; people were already sinners. But the law gave "the knowledge of sin" by defining the sins already in the human heart.

Righteousness Apart from the Law

Not only will the deeds of the law provide no justification, "the righteousness of God apart from the law is revealed, being witnessed by the Law and the Prophets" (Romans 3:21). The Hebrew Scriptures foretold the coming of the new covenant, which would be radically different from the Mosaic covenant and which would provide soteriological righteousness with no reference to the law of Moses.

"Behold, the days are coming, says the LORD, when I will make a new covenant with the house of Israel and with the house of Judah—not according to the covenant that I made with their fathers in the day that I took them by the hand to bring them out of the land of Egypt, My covenant which they broke, though I was a husband to them, says the LORD" (Jeremiah 31:31-32).

In New Testament terms, this new covenant would result in justification, regeneration, and sanctification:

"Then I will sprinkle clean water on you, and you shall be clean; I will cleanse you from all your filthiness and from all your idols. I will give you a new heart and put a new spirit within you; I will take the heart of stone out of your flesh and give you a heart of flesh. I will put My Spirit within you and cause you to walk in My statutes, and you will keep My judgments and do them" (Ezekiel 36:25-27).

Justification is described by the words "I will sprinkle clean water on you, and you shall be clean; I will cleanse you from all your filthiness and from all your idols." The new covenant would make provision for believers to receive forgiveness of their sins and to gain right standing with God. Regeneration is promised in the words "I will give you a new heart and put a new spirit within you; I will take the heart of stone out of your flesh and give you a heart of flesh. I will put My Spirit within you." By the new covenant, believers would actually be made into new persons—regenerated—by the Spirit of God. Sanctification is described in the words "I will . . . cause you to walk in My statutes, and you will keep My judgments and do them." The new covenant enables the believer to be obedient to the commandments of God.

The covenant established at Sinai did not make these provisions: "Yet the Lord has not given you a heart to perceive and eyes to see and ears to hear, to this very day" (Deuteronomy 29:4). The prophecies in the Hebrew Scriptures about the coming of a new covenant required the passing away of the old covenant. The new covenant is by definition something *apart from* the law. It is not a further development of the law or another form of the law; it is a different covenant altogether.

Boasting Is Excluded

The law of Moses was a "law of works." (See Romans 10:5; Galatians 3:12.) "Where is boasting then? It is excluded. By what law? Of works? No, but by the law of faith" (Romans 3:27). Due to the nature of the new covenant, there is no room for Jewish boasting of superiority over other believers. If the old covenant had still been in effect, there could have been a place for boasting, for the old covenant rewarded performance. Those who adhered to the commands of the law of Moses could thus boast in their obedience. Paul himself had boasted in his adherence to the law prior to his conversion (Philippians 3:4-7). But the radical difference between the old and new covenants is seen here: the old covenant was a law of works; the new covenant is a law of faith. If a person is justified by faith, he has no room to boast; he has done nothing. What he has received was given to him as a free gift.

Justification Apart from the Law

Justification by faith comes apart from the deeds of the law: "Therefore we conclude that a man is justified by faith apart from the deeds of the law" (Romans 3:28). (See also Romans 3:21.) Here again we see the fundamental difference between the two covenants. The new covenant is not a continuation or further development of the covenant established at Sinai. The justification that comes by faith is *apart from* the law of Moses. On the basis of exclusive faith in Jesus Christ, people will be counted righteous in the eyes of God.

The Law Established

To this point the Roman letter has so strongly argued for the termination of the law of Moses that it anticipates a question Jewish readers would ask: "Do we then make void the law through faith?" (Romans 3:31a). This question underscores that the new covenant had replaced the old covenant. No lesser argument would give birth to this kind of question.

It may seem surprising, in view of the assertion that the law has terminated (see Romans 3:21, 28), that the response to this question was, "Certainly not! On the contrary, we establish the law" (Romans 3:31b). Does this answer mean, after all, that the law of Moses is still in effect, that the old covenant has not been replaced, and that people are still under obligation to the 613 commandments given to Moses?

To use Paul's words, "Certainly not!" The Book of

Romans does not, in one breath, assert the termination of the law and its replacement by the new covenant, and in the next breath declare that the law is still in effect. It is important to note that the question is not, "Is the law still in effect?" The question is, "Since we are justified by *faith*, does this make the law *void*?" *Katargeo*, translated "void," means "to make ineffective, nullify." *Histanomen*, translated "establish," means "to establish, confirm." Here is the point: The law of Moses was given for specific reasons to ancient Israel. That it has now been replaced by the new covenant does not nullify the reasons the law was originally given; it has served its purposes and accomplished its legitimate goals. Thus, the validity of the law is confirmed. It was a valid covenant; its purposes have been achieved. It was not given in vain.

J. Dwight Pentecost listed ten purposes for the law of Moses: (1) to reveal the holiness of God; (2) to reveal or expose the sinfulness of man; (3) to reveal the standard of holiness required of those in fellowship with a holy God; (4) to supervise the physical, mental, and spiritual development of the redeemed Israelite until he came to maturity in the Lord; (5) to be the unifying principle that made possible the establishment of the nation; (6) to separate Israel from the nations in order that they might become a kingdom of priests; (7) to make provision for forgiveness of sins and restoration to fellowship; (8) to make provision for a redeemed people to worship; (9) to provide a test as to whether one was in the kingdom or the theocracy over which God ruled; and (10) to reveal Jesus Christ.[5] Robert P. Lightner distilled the matter down ever further, offering five purposes for the law of Moses: (1) to reveal God's holiness; (2) to unify and distinguish

Israel as a nation; (3) to provide a basis for Israel's walk with and worship of God; (4) to expose the sinfulness of man; and (5) to reveal Christ.[6]

The law of Moses excelled in accomplishing its intended purposes. To that end it is established or confirmed as a legitimate covenant given by God to a specific people to achieve certain goals. But that does not mean it is still binding on believers; Romans repeatedly asserts its conclusion and replacement by the new covenant.

A Faith Promise

When God established the Abrahamic covenant with Abraham, it had nothing to do with the law of Moses. The law of Moses was four centuries in the future. (See Galatians 3:13-18.) "For the promise that he would be the heir of the world was not to Abraham or to his seed through the law, but through the righteousness of faith" (Romans 4:13). For a complete account of the Abrahamic covenant, see Genesis 12:1-4; 13:14-17; 15:1-18; 17:1-8. The basis upon which God made this covenant with Abraham was faith, not law. The law was added later—not added to the Abrahamic covenant (Galatians 3:15, 17), but added to the requirements God made of national Israel—for a specific reason and for a limited period of time (Galatians 3:19-25). The reason was Israel's sinfulness, and the time extended only to the coming of the Messiah.

Law Versus Faith

Romans 4:14 reveals the contrast between law and faith: "For if those who are of the law are heirs, faith is made void and the promise made of no effect." If a person received the provisions of the Abrahamic covenant by adhering to the law of Moses, neither faith nor God's promise to Abraham would have any meaning. The law is not a faith system; it is a works system. God counted Abraham righteous because of his faith, not his works. (See Romans 4:2-5.) The promises God made to Abraham were not predicated on obedience to the law; Abraham knew nothing of the law. If we now say that in order to participate in the Abrahamic covenant one must embrace the law of Moses, we are adding conditions God never intended, and we are changing the Abrahamic covenant from a faith system to a works system. (Compare Galatians 3:13-18.)

Law Produces Wrath

"The law brings about wrath; for where there is no law there is no transgression" (Romans 4:15). By nature, the law produces wrath, or the judicial judgment of God upon sin. The law of Moses was precise in detailing sin. Since it contained 613 commandments, it essentially described 613 ways to sin. There is something about the sin nature inherited from Adam that is provoked by law to further sin. (See Romans 7:5, 13.) In some ways, it is like the little boy whose mother says, "Whatever you do, don't get in the cookie jar before dinner." Once the boy has been warned, however, he has only one thing on his mind: figuring out a way to get into the cookie jar without being caught. There is something perverse about human nature that prompts a person to see just what he can get away with. This is why, when some people see a sign proclaiming, "Wet Paint," they will invariably touch the paint to see if it really is wet.

In addition, since there is no transgression where

there is no law (Romans 5:13), the law of Moses produced many more opportunities for people to experience the wrath of God.

Faith, Grace, and a Sure Promise

The promise given to Abraham came through faith: "Therefore it is of faith that it might be according to grace, so that the promise might be sure to all the seed, not only to those who are of the law, but also to those who are of the faith of Abraham, who is the father of us all" (Romans 4:16). The blessings contained in the Abrahamic covenant come by grace, or as a free gift of God. Thus, *all* of Abraham's seed (Romans 4:11-12), Jews and Gentiles, are certain to receive the blessing of Abraham, provided they "are of the faith of Abraham, who is the father of us all" (believing Jews and Gentiles). (See John 8:39; Galatians 3:13-14.) This does not mean Christians become "spiritual Jews." Such a term never appears in Scripture. But it does mean that whether a person is a Jew or a Gentile, if he is a person of faith, he can look to Abraham as his father.

No Law: No Imputation of Sin

Romans 5:13-17 forms a lengthy parenthetical statement. We can gain a basic understanding of the entire passage by going immediately from verse 12 to verse 18. Just as Adam's sin results in the condemnation of all humanity, so the atonement by Jesus Christ provides justification to all humanity.

This parenthetical statement explains the situation prior to the law of Moses (verses 13-14) and the superiority of Christ's atonement over Adam's sin (verses 15-17).

From Adam's sin until the law of Moses, human beings shared universally in the sin nature, or the state of spiritual separation from God. Their inherent sinfulness was demonstrated profusely. (See Genesis 6:5.) But since the law of Moses had not been given and could not therefore serve its purpose of defining sin, many individual sins committed by people, which would later be defined as sin in the law of Moses, were not reckoned to their account before God: "For until the law sin was in the world, but sin is not imputed where there is no law" (Romans 5:13). (See also Romans 4:15; 7:7.)

This statement does not mean these people were saved by ignorance; Romans has already pointed out that those who did not have the law failed to live up to the limited revelation they had. (See Romans 1:18-32.) What it does mean is that nobody prior to the law of Moses will be held responsible for the requirements of the law of Moses. They will, however, be held responsible for the sins they committed against the revelation they did have.

Some have suggested that prior to the law of Moses, no sins were reckoned to the accounts of people at all. But this theory does not fit the facts of Scripture. God certainly held Cain responsible for his personal sins, and God apparently provided him with a sin offering, for He said to Cain, "If you do well, will you not be accepted? And if you do not do well, sin lies at the door. And its desire is for you, but you should rule over it" (Genesis 4:7). In the Hebrew language, the same word refers to "sin" and "sin offering," emphasizing the complete identity of a person's sin with the sacrifice offered for the sin. Genesis 4:7 seems to imply that, somewhat as when God provided a ram for Abraham to offer instead of Isaac, God provided a sin offering for Cain to sacrifice. At any rate, Job without question offered sin offerings on behalf of his children (Job 1:5), and he lived prior to the law of Moses.

Romans 5:13 indicates that the only sins actually reckoned to a person's account are those he commits against revelation. But this does not mean anyone will be saved because he did the best they knew to do; Romans 1-3 conclusively proves in that no one actually does the best he knows to do. All people sin by failing to live up to the revelation given them.

The Law's Purpose

We can deduce from Scripture many purposes of the law of Moses.[7] Romans 5:20 points out one of them: the law of Moses was given to emphasize the reality of sin. Grammatically, the phrase "that the offense might abound" can be a purpose clause or a result clause. In other words, it can refer to the purpose for which the law was given or the result of the law being given. Regardless of which meaning we choose, the law of Moses revealed and aroused sinful passions. (See Romans 7:5-11.) People were already sinners, but the law exposed the sin problem.

God intended to demonstrate without question the universal sinfulness of humanity, so that all people would recognize their need of a Savior. (See Galatians 3:19-25.) Although the law of Moses made it very clear that all were sinners, the grace of God surpassed human sinfulness in providing salvation.

Not under Law

The Christian is not under law, but grace: "For sin shall not have dominion over you, for you are not under law but under grace. What then? Shall we sin because we are not under law but under grace? Certainly not!" (Romans 6:14-15). The believer's union with Christ results in the destruction of sin's dominion. The issue here is not whether a believer can be tempted or whether he may commit specific acts of sin. The issue is whether sin must continue to rule the believer.

Here we find in microcosm the relationship between the old covenant (the law of Moses) and the new covenant. For those who were under the law of Moses, the law itself aroused sinful passions (Romans 7:5). One purpose of the law was to make sin exceedingly sinful (Romans 7:13). That is, the law illustrated the helplessness of man to free himself from sin's dominion by merely trying to adhere to high codes of conduct. The point of this verse is that if believers were under the law of Moses, sin would have dominion over them. But since they are under grace, sin's ruling power is broken. The law demanded perfect obedience and thereby heightened the sin problem, whereas grace gives the believer both the desire and the ability to do what is right. (See Philippians 2:13; I Corinthians 15:10.)

Speaking from the standpoint of human wisdom (verse 19), Paul asked a question reminiscent of Romans 6:1. Does freedom from the law of Moses mean the believer should sin profusely? Again, Paul denied this with the strong *me genoito*, translated "God forbid" in the KJV and "Certainly not" in the NKJV.

The phrase "under the law" appears eight other times in the New Testament. (See Romans 3:19; I Corinthians 9:20-21; Galatians 3:23; 4:4-5, 21; 5:18.) An examination of each appearance of the phrase reveals that to be "under the law" means to be obligated to it as a way of life. It does not mean that anyone, including the Jews during the era of the old covenant, ever received soteriological justification by adherence to the law. (See Acts 13:39; Galatians 3:21.)

Paul wrote, "To the Jews I became as a Jew, that I might win Jews; to those who are under the law, as under the law, that I might win those who are under the law" (I Corinthians 9:20). Paul did not mean that, after receiving the gift of righteousness by faith in Jesus Christ, he reverted to the law of Moses as the source of righteousness. Indeed, he counted as rubbish all that he had formerly depended upon to commend him to God. (See Philippians 3:4-9.) Those who reverted to the law of Moses as a means of earning favor with God, and who preached this as the way of salvation, were "accursed," "evil workers," and "dogs" (Galatians 1:8-9; Philippians 3:2). When Paul became "as under the law" in order to win those who were "under the law," he voluntarily, though unnecessarily and temporarily, embraced the law of Moses as a way of life so as to avoid offending the non-Christian Jewish people he was attempting to reach with the gospel. (See Acts 21:17-26.)

That Christians are not under the law means they have no obligation to the law as a way of life. Instead, the Christian way of life is characterized by grace.

The Law Gives No Power over Sin

Romans 7 explains why the believer is free from obligation to the old covenant, the law of Moses. But, in terminology that has puzzled many, Paul dramatically asserted his struggles with specific temptations to sin. His candid revelations offer hope to the readers; if he found victory over sin and condemnation, they can too.

Romans 7:1 directly addresses Jewish readers, using an example from the law of Moses: "Or do you not know, brethren (for I speak to those who know the law), that the law has dominion over a man as long as he lives?" When the law of Moses was in effect, the only way a Jewish person could find relief from its demands was in death. The law governed every minute detail of the life of the Jewish people, from birth until death.

Though the main point in this chapter does not have to do with marriage laws, it uses the law regulating marriage to illustrate the basis upon which believers today are freed from obligation to the law of Moses: "For the woman who has a husband is bound by the law to her husband as long as he lives. But if the husband dies, she is released from the law of her husband" (Romans 7:2). Although the law of Moses made provisions for divorce (Deuteronomy 24:1; Matthew 5:31; 19:7), God's original intention was for marriage to be for life (Genesis 2:24). Only death was intended to release a woman from her covenant obligations to her husband.

Since marriage was ideally for life, if a woman married another man while her husband was still alive, she would be identified as an adulteress: "So then if, while her husband lives, she marries another man, she will be called an adulteress; but if her husband dies, she is free from that law, so that she is no adulteress, though she has married another man" (Romans 7:3). Since the point here is not to give detailed teaching about every scenario in marriage conflicts, this passage does not address possible justifications for divorce, but silence here does not negate the teaching on this subject in other sections of

Scripture. (See Matthew 19:7; I Corinthians 7:10-28.) The purpose here is to demonstrate the basis upon which believers are free from the law of Moses, using the example of a woman who is legally free from her covenant obligations to her husband upon his death.

Just like a woman whose husband dies, believers who are in union with Christ have "become dead to the law": "Therefore, my brethren, you also have become dead to the law through the body of Christ, that you may be married to another, even to Him who was raised from the dead, that we should bear fruit to God" (Romans 7:4). The death of Jesus Christ terminated the law's dominion (Romans 10:4), and those who identify with Him in His death (see Romans 6:3-5) are thereby released from obligation to the law. It was necessary that they be released from obligation to the law so that they might "be married to another," Jesus Christ. The believer cannot be obligated to two covenants at once; there can be no mixing of covenants or dividing of loyalties. God intended marriage to be monogamous, and on the same basis only one of the two covenants can be in effect at one time.

Under the old covenant, sin ruled and produced greater sinfulness. (See Romans 6:5, 13.) The law did not produce the fruit of life; it resulted in death (Romans 6:21). But the new covenant is radically different; those who are identified with Christ "bear fruit to God." (See Romans 6:22.)

The Epistles use the term "flesh" in many different contexts, usually to describe some aspect of human nature (not just the physical body). Ordinarily, "flesh" means human nature as marred by sin, or the sin principle that dwells in everyone as a consequence of Adam's fall. (See Romans 5:12.) But we must always remember that words are defined by their contexts.

The word "flesh" in Romans 7:5 is contextually defined as pertaining to the time when Jews were under the law of Moses: "For when we were in the flesh, the passions of sins which were aroused by the law were at work in our members to bear fruit to death." In this case, to say, "For when we were in the flesh" is equivalent to saying, "For when we were under the law." (See verses 1-6.) The era of the law was the era of the "flesh"; the era of the new covenant is the era of the "Spirit." (See Romans 8:9.)

The Epistle to the Galatians uses the word "flesh" in a similar way. (See Galatians 3:1-5.) The law was, in this sense, a "flesh" covenant because it focused on works, on the ability of people to conform perfectly to its demands. In other words, the law demanded that people obey on the basis of their own human strength; it offered no help from the Spirit.

Paul's statement, "*When* we were in the flesh [i.e., under the law]," underscores that the era of the law was over; a new era had begun. Believers are no longer under the law. (See Romans 6:14-15.)

The experience of those who were under the law was that the law, with its high and demanding standards, aroused "sinful passions." In other words, the law did not curb the sins it forbade; it actually provoked people to greater sin. (See Romans 6:13.) Sin's strong desires worked in the "members" of those who were under the law to produce separation from God (death). (See Romans 6:12, 19.) The law of Moses, the old covenant, did not have within itself the ability to draw people to God; the sin nature took advantage of this weakness of the law to drive them away from God.

The law showed people their imperfections, their unworthiness, but it made no provision for them to overcome their unworthiness and to be restored to right standing in the eyes of God. (See Hebrews 10:1-4, 11; Galatians 2:16.) Even if a person had been theoretically able to perfectly obey all 613 commandments of the law of Moses from the day he was born until the day he died, this would not given him right standing with God. During the law, just as in every other age, the only way to right standing with God was by faith. (See Romans 4:6-8; Hebrews 11:39.)

With the coming of Jesus Christ, the law of Moses was terminated: "But now we have been delivered from the law, having died to what we were held by, so that we should serve in the newness of the Spirit and not in the oldness of the letter" (Romans 7:6). Those who were under the law are now delivered from it through their identification with Jesus Christ in His death. (See Romans 6:2-8; 7:4.) With the passing away of the old covenant and the institution of the new covenant, it is now possible to serve God "in the newness of the Spirit and not in the oldness of the letter."

Due to the provisions of the new covenant, people no longer relate to God on the basis of "the letter," or the law of Moses (see II Corinthians 3:6-7), but on the basis of the presence of the Holy Spirit within them. Under the old covenant, people struggled to conform to the letter of the law in order to please God. This was an impossible task.

But under the new covenant, God places the righteousness of Jesus Christ on the believer's account, reckoning the believer to be as pleasing to Him as Jesus is (II

Corinthians 5:21), and on that basis the believer receives the free gift of the Holy Spirit. Thus the service new covenant believers render to God comes from the perspective that they are *already* pleasing to Him; it is the natural consequence of their acceptance by Him and of the intimate relationship they enjoy with Him by their union with Christ.

This is radically different from the service offered to God under "the oldness of the letter [the law]." That service sprang from a desperate but hopeless effort to conform; new covenant service springs from an understanding of God's full acceptance of the believer coupled with the power of the Holy Spirit.

Does the weakness of the law mean that the law itself was sinful? Again we find the strongest possible denial: "What shall we say then? Is the law sin? Certainly not! On the contrary, I would not have known sin except through the law. For I would not have known covetousness unless the law had said, 'You shall not covet'" (Romans 7:7). The law itself was holy, just and good (verse 12). It held up a perfect standard; it clearly defined sin. The only problem with the law was that it demanded perfect obedience but did not empower anyone to meet its demands. (See Romans 8:3.) "The law was given through Moses, but grace and truth came through Jesus Christ" (John 1:17). Law does not enable anyone to obey; enablement to do right comes only through the grace of God and the work of the Spirit. (See John 15:5; I Corinthians 15:10; Philippians 2:13.)

Romans 7:7 explains a major purpose of the law of Moses: to define sin clearly. Paul did not mean he would not have known *about* sin, except for the law. Nor did he mean he would never have coveted were it not for the law. What he meant is that he would have been unable to *identify* sin, or to put a specific label on it, were it not for the law. Because of the law's specific definition of coveting, for example, Paul was able to identify the nature of his sin. (See Exodus 20:17.)

Beginning in Romans 7:7 and throughout the remainder of the chapter, Paul used the personal pronoun "I" as opposed to his earlier use of "we," "you," and "he." Thus he now discussed his personal experiences, which are, of course, typical of the experiences of all believers. Paul's use of the personal pronoun makes his observations more helpful and easier to receive. If he experienced these struggles and was successful in rising above them, so can we.

Although the law defined sin, it did not aid in conquering temptation: "But sin, taking opportunity by the commandment, produced in me all manner of evil desire. For apart from the law sin was dead" (Romans 7:8). The sin nature took advantage of the specific commandments in the law of Moses to produce "all manner of evil desire." It seems inherent in sinful human nature to desire forbidden fruit. (See Proverbs 9:17-18.) Because of its long list of forbidden activities, the law of Moses actually suggested sinful activities some people may never have considered. Once the idea is suggested by its prohibition, however, the sin nature takes advantage of the thought to produce evil desires. In context, the statement "apart from the law sin was dead" means that until the law suggested specific sinful activities by prohibiting them, Paul had no awareness of those sins.

Paul wrote, "I was alive once without the law, but

when the commandment came, sin revived and I died" (Romans 7:9). When was Paul "alive once without the law"? When did the commandment (not to covet, verse 7) come, resulting in sin coming to life and producing death in Paul? The most reasonable answer seems to be that Paul discussed his childhood, his time of innocence before he became aware of his own sinfulness and of the demands of the law.

Every Jewish boy experiences his bar mitzvah, a ceremony conducted at age thirteen as a rite of passage into adulthood. The very words describing this ceremony mean "son of the commandment." After the bar mitzvah, the Jewish boy is considered to be fully responsible to obey the law of Moses. Perhaps Paul had this thought in mind when he wrote the words of this verse. As a youth, Paul probably enjoyed fellowship with God to the extent possible under the old covenant, but when he became aware of his sinfulness and of his inability to conform perfectly to the law's high standard, he "died," or experienced separation from fellowship with God.

Though the law of Moses was intended to show Israel how to live, Paul found it to produce death, or separation from God: "And the commandment, which was to bring life, I found to bring death" (Romans 7:10). This verse demonstrates that demanding right behavior from those who are not recipients of the grace of God is ultimately unsuccessful. Such demands merely compound their problem and drive them further into hopelessness and despair.

In a statement similar to verse 8, Paul pointed out that sin took advantage of the law of Moses to deceive him and to separate him from fellowship with God: "For sin, taking occasion by the commandment, deceived me, and by it killed me" (Romans 7:11). This is similar to Eve's experience: she was deceived and "fell into transgression" (I Timothy 2:14). The word translated "deceived" means "to lead astray." The sin nature takes advantage of prohibitions to create within a person a desire for the forbidden. (See Romans 7:5, 8.) By doing this, it leads the person away from the obedience intended by the law and separates him from God.

So far as the law itself is concerned, it is holy, and the commandment not to covet is holy, just, and good (Romans 7:7, 12). We cannot fault the law, if we consider it in and of itself; however, it does not enable people to conform to its codes. (See Romans 8:3.)

Does separation from God result from the law itself? The response to this question is strong: "Has then what is good become death to me? Certainly not! But sin, that it might appear sin, was producing death in me through what is good, so that sin through the commandment might become exceedingly sinful" (Romans 7:13). The law, in and of itself, does not separate people from God, but the sin nature in all human beings takes advantage of the law to produce even more sin, and thus to separate people from God. (See Romans 7:5.) Here we see another major purpose of the law: it clearly points out the sinfulness of people and their inability to please God by their own strength.

The law itself is spiritual: "For we know that the law is spiritual" (Romans 7:14). It is a perfect standard; we can find no fault with it. But all human beings share Paul's problem: they are "carnal," that is, they share in the sin nature that springs from Adam. "But I am carnal, sold under sin" (Romans 7:14b). (See Romans 5:12.) Because of the universal sin nature, human beings are "sold under sin." That is, they are slaves to sin. (See Romans 6:17, 19-20.)

Paul's struggles, as described beginning at Romans 7:15 and through the end of the chapter, are those of a regenerate man who attempts to live victoriously over the sin principle by the power of his own human abilities or by reliance upon the law of Moses: "For what I am doing, I do not understand. For what I will to do, that I do not practice; but what I hate, that I do" (Romans 7:15). We see Paul's emphasis in this section on self-reliance by his repeated use of the first person personal pronoun "I," as contrasted with his infrequent use of it in Romans 6 (which identifies union with Christ in His death and resurrection as the way to victory over sin) and Romans 8 (which emphasizes the work of the Holy Spirit on behalf of the believer). Paul found that when he relied on his own abilities, or tried to relate to God on the basis of the law, he could not understand his own actions. Self-reliance seemed to produce in Paul an almost schizophrenic condition: On the one hand, he willed to do right, but he failed to practice what he willed. He engaged in practices he hated.

This will always be the experience of any person who attempts to please God by self-effort or by reliance on the law of Moses or any similar works-dominated system. Nothing else can result, or it could be said that we save ourselves. Since salvation is a gift, it comes by grace through faith, it is not of ourselves, and it is not the result of works. (See Ephesians 2:8-9.) When a person relies on his own ability or on the law, he will experience the frustrations described in this chapter.

Paul's inability to actually practice what he willed to do demonstrated the accuracy of the law of Moses: "If, then, I do what I will not to do, I agree with the law that it is good" (Romans 7:16). The law declared sin to be sin by defining it, and it declared sinners to be sinners by revealing their inability to attain perfection. (See Romans 7:5-13.)

The reason for man's inability to do what is right by his own power is the sin nature that dwells in every person: "But now, it is no longer I who do it, but sin that dwells in me" (Romans 7:17). The sin nature interacts with the law to produce ever increasing sinfulness in man. (See Romans 7:5, 8.)

Paul confessed that nothing good resided in his human nature as it was marred by sin: "For I know that in me (that is, in my flesh) nothing good dwells; for to will is present with me, but how to perform what is good I do not find. For the good that I will to do, I do not do; but the evil I will not to do, that I practice" (Romans 7:18-19). This observation agrees with the previous statement of the universal sinfulness of humanity. (See Romans 3:10-18.)

This passage does not discuss the Holy Spirit, which dwells within the regenerated human spirit, but the Adamic nature shared by all humans. The Adamic nature allows a person to *will* what is right, but it does not give him the power to actually do right as a way of life. When a person relies on the power of the indwelling Holy Spirit, he has the ability both to *will* and to *do* right (Philippians 2:13), but when he relies only upon his own human ability, though he can will, he cannot do.

In a restatement of Romans 7:17, Paul asserted that his inability to do right was a result of the indwelling sin nature inherited from Adam: "Now if I do what I will not to do, it is no longer I who do it, but sin that dwells in me" (Romans 7:20).

The Book of Romans discusses six laws. They are (1) the law of Moses (3:19); (2) the principle of law, without specific identification with the Mosaic code (3:21); (3) the law of faith (3:27); (4) the law of sin (7:21, 23, 25); (5) the law of the mind (7:16, 23); and (6) the law of the Spirit (8:2, 4).

Romans 7:21 describes the law of the indwelling sin nature, which conquers the law of the mind (verse 23): "I find then a law, that evil is present with me, the one who wills to do good." The fall of man in the Garden of Eden did not completely destroy man's desire to do right (the law of the mind), but it did infuse him so powerfully with the sin nature that he is unable to do right consistently.

Paul wrote, "For I delight in the law of God according to the inward man" (Romans 7:22). Contextually, the "inward man" is the mind (Romans 7:23). As far as his mind was concerned, Paul would have been delighted to have been able to conform perfectly to the law of Moses. But the law of sin conquers the law of the mind and captures the individual: "But I see another law in my members, warring against the law of my mind, and bringing me into captivity to the law of sin which is in my members" (Romans 7:23). (See Romans 7:5, 8.)

The only result that can come from self-reliance or attempting to relate to God on the basis of the law is desperate frustration. Paul was driven to cry out for deliverance from his wretched condition: "O wretched man that

I am! Who will deliver me from this body of death?" (Romans 7:24). "The body of death" is human nature as it is marred by sin. (See Romans 6:6.) The sin nature abuses one's human existence to produce separation from God (death). (See Romans 6:12-13, 19; 7:5, 13; 8:10.)

After such a seemingly hopeless situation as the preceding verses describe, welcome relief comes: deliverance from the domination of the sin nature is available through Jesus Christ our Lord. "I thank God—through Jesus Christ our Lord! So then, with the mind I myself serve the law of God, but with the flesh the law of sin" (Romans 7:25).

Romans 6 describes this relief as coming through union with Christ in His death, burial, and resurrection. Romans 8 describes the relief that comes through the indwelling Holy Spirit.

Paul concluded Romans 7 by restating that as long as he relied on his own ability or attempted to relate to God on the basis of the law, he could have the right desires, but he could not do the right things. Until believers are transformed into the glorious likeness of Jesus Christ (I John 3:2; I Corinthians 15:51-57; Philippians 3:20-21), this will be their experience. The only way a believer can live in victory over the sin nature is to rely exclusively on his union with Christ and on the indwelling Spirit.

Two Laws

Even though Paul consistently declared the termination of the law of Moses, he was not antinomian ("against law"). That is, he was not opposed to the idea of law altogether. Instead, he recognized that there is a new law: "For the law of the Spirit of life in Christ Jesus has made me free from the law of sin and death" (Romans 8:2). "The law of the Spirit of life in Christ Jesus" has to do with Jesus Christ's baptizing those who believe on Him with the Holy Spirit. (See Matthew 3:11; Mark 1:8; Luke 3:16; John 1:33; Acts 2:33.) The Holy Spirit is the "Spirit of life." Since the death resulting from sin is separation from fellowship with God, "life" here is restoration to fellowship with God.

This new law frees the believer from "the law of sin and death." This is apparently a reference to the sin principle (Romans 7:20, 25), which results in separation from God. It may also be an allusion to the way the sin nature takes advantage of the law of Moses to compound sin and thus to separate a person from God. (See Romans 7:5, 8-11; 8:3.)

God Sent His Son

Though the law of Moses was holy (Romans 7:12), it had an inherent weakness: "For what the law could not do in that it was weak through the flesh, God did by sending His own Son in the likeness of sinful flesh, on account of sin: He condemned sin in the flesh" (Romans 8:3). It was weak "through the flesh," that is, it made no provision for human nature being marred by sin and for human beings being thus incapable of attaining a standard of perfection by their own strength. What the law of Moses could not do was to impute righteousness. What the law could not do, God accomplished by the Incarnation.

God sent His own Son in the *likeness* of sinful flesh. Although the flesh, or human nature, of Jesus was genuine humanity received from His human mother, Mary, verse 3 uses the word "likeness" because Jesus was spared the sin nature by virtue of the virgin birth. He had no human father; the Holy Spirit brought about His conception. A statement that God sent His Son "in sinful flesh" would compromise the sinlessness of Christ, while saying that God sent His Son "in the likeness of flesh" would compromise the humanity of Christ. The wording of verse 3 precisely communicates the truth of the Incarnation: Jesus Christ is genuinely and completely human, but—like the first Adam originally—He did not possess the sin nature.

Jesus Christ, as God incarnate, is the Son of God sent into the world. (See I Timothy 3:16; John 3:17; 7:33; 17:18; 20:21; Galatians 4:4-6.) This does not mean He preexisted the Incarnation *as the Son*. He certainly did preexist the Incarnation, but *as the Word*, which is God Himself. (See John 1:1-2, 14; I John 1:1-2.) John's use of "Word" (*Logos*) does not imply existence separate from God or even plurality of persons within God; rather, it is reminiscent of Genesis 1, where God created by His Word. God is the being of ultimate integrity, and His Word cannot be separated from Him as having a conscious existence apart from Him, any more than the life of God can be separated from Him.[8] Psalm 29:3-8 equates the voice of God with God Himself. The Targums (Aramaic paraphrases of the Hebrew Scriptures) use the word *memra*, Aramaic for "word," for God Himself. The Son's being "sent" does not demand preexistence *as the Son* any more than the sending of John the Baptist (John 1:6) implies his preexistence.

The Son of God was sent "on account of sin." His premier mission was redemption; Jesus came to solve the sin problem once and for all. (See John 1:29; I Corinthians

5:7; I John 2:2; Hebrews 10:12; Revelation 13:8.) Whereas sin had previously condemned all people, Jesus dealt with sin by turning the tables on it: He condemned sin. To condemn means to judge; Jesus provided the final judgment of sin on the cross of Calvary. (See Colossians 2:14-15.)

He did this "in the flesh," or in His genuine human existence. On the cross, Jesus did not rely on His deity in any way to avoid the suffering associated with His substitutionary death. Although on the cross He was God manifested in the flesh, just as He was and is at all points of His existence, through His humanity He humbled Himself to the point of death, and to the most despicable death known in the Roman Empire at the time, death on a cross. (See Philippians 2:8.)

Fulfilling the Law's Righteous Requirement

The reason God sent His Son was "that the righteous requirement of the law might be fulfilled in us who do not walk according to the flesh but according to the Spirit" (Romans 8:4). At first glance, it may seem as if this verse contradicts the idea that the coming of Christ negated the law of Moses. (See Romans 7:4; 10:4; Galatians 3:23-25; Hebrews 10:9.) However, it does not say "the *law* might be fulfilled *by* us," but "the righteous *requirement* of the law might be fulfilled *in* us." The word translated "might be fulfilled" (Greek, *plerothei*) is the first aorist passive subjunctive of *pleroo*, a word commonly used in the New Testament to refer to the fulfillment of prophecy. (See Matthew 1:22; 5:17-18.) Since it is in the passive voice, it describes the subject—those of us who do not walk according to the flesh but according to the Spirit—as receiving the action of the verb. In other words, by some action outside ourselves—in this case the Atonement (verse 3)—the righteous requirement of the law can be fulfilled in us.

The verse does not specify what the righteous requirement of the law is, but it may refer to the judgment of sin (Romans 8:3). That is, the law of Moses required that sin be judged, and Jesus Christ accomplished this on the cross. (See II Corinthians 5:21.) Romans 3:21-26 teaches that Jesus Christ, by His blood, is our propitiation—the satisfaction of the righteous judgment of God on sin. By virtue of His righteousness He both justifies and sanctifies those who have faith in Him.

Some may think that the phrase "who do not walk according to the flesh but according to the Spirit" is a conditional clause, indicating that the fulfillment of the righteous requirement of the law depends upon our success in walking according to the Spirit rather than according to the flesh. But there is no subjunctive (conditional element) in this phrase. It is a simple statement of fact: Believers do not walk according to the flesh; they walk according to the Spirit.

The first phrase in the verse ("that the righteous requirement of the law might be fulfilled in us") is in the subjunctive mood, indicating there is a condition, but the condition for the fulfilling of the law's righteous requirement in us is the Atonement, which Jesus Christ met and which we must apply personally to our lives. The latter part of verse 4 indicates that since believers are filled with the Holy Spirit, they draw strength from the Spirit, not from the flesh. The word "flesh" may refer to life under the law of Moses, while "according to the Spirit" refers to life under the new covenant.[9]

The Carnal Mind

The word "carnal" is synonymous with "flesh." Both are translated from the same Greek word, *sarx*. Paul wrote, "Because the carnal mind is enmity against God; for it is not subject to the law of God, nor indeed can be. So then, those who are in the flesh cannot please God" (Romans 8:7-8). The carnal, or fleshly, mind is against God. Not only does it not submit to the law of God, it is impossible for it to submit to the law of God. The "law of God" here is is not necessarily a reference to the law of Moses; it may refer to anything God demands. There is no point in an unregenerate person attempting to behave like a regenerate person; it is impossible for him to conform himself to God's requirements. The only way a person can be subject to God's law and thus to please God is to be regenerate, to be born again (John 3:5), which is the same as being "in the Spirit."

The Law Belonged to Israel

Romans 9:4 speaks of the "Israelites, to whom pertain the adoption, the glory, the covenants, the giving of the law, the service of God, and the promises." Among other things that are uniquely Jewish is the law of Moses. Theologians consider the law of Moses to be one of the eight covenants,[10] but it was such a preeminent covenant and so unique in its purpose that Scripture considers it separately here. (See Deuteronomy 5:1-22.)

Some scholars question whether the Palestinian covenant was a separate covenant or merely an extension of the Mosaic covenant. In any event, it was exclusively for national Israel. Although the Abrahamic, Davidic and new covenants pertain to Israel, believing Gentiles enjoy certain benefits from each of them. From the Abrahamic covenant, believing Gentiles receive justification by faith (Galatians 3:14). From the Davidic covenant, which included the promise to David that the Messiah would come as his offspring (Acts 2:29-31), Gentiles are invited to believe on the Jewish Messiah (Isaiah 11:10). From the new covenant, Gentiles receive cleansing from sin by the blood of Jesus, and they receive the gift of the Holy Spirit (Matthew 26:27-28; I John 2:2; Acts 2:17).

But God gave the law of Moses exclusively to the nation of Israel; He did not give it to the Gentile nations of the world, and He never intended for Gentiles to adhere to it or receive its blessing. (See Psalm 147:19-20; Acts 15:5, 24; Galatians 3-5.) When Romans 9:4 singles out the law of Moses, separating it from the covenants just mentioned, it serves the literary purpose of putting the law of Moses in a category by itself; it was exclusively for the nation of Israel.

Stumbling at the Stumbling Stone

The great mistake of Israel in New Testament times is that they attempted to attain righteousness by the works of the law of Moses: "But Israel, pursuing the law of righteousness, has not attained to the law of righteousness. Why? Because they did not seek it by faith, but as it were by the works of the law. For they stumbled at that stumbling stone" (Romans 9:31-32)). In contrast to Gentiles who attained righteousness by putting their faith in Jesus Christ (Romans 9:30), ancient Israel focused, not on the Messiah as the one who would satisfy the righteous requirements of the law on their behalf, but on the law itself as a means of achieving righteousness.

Their pursuit of righteousness was not by faith, but by works. Thus they stumbled at Jesus Christ, the stumbling stone about whom the Hebrew Scriptures prophesied. (See Psalm 118:22; Isaiah 8:14; 28:16.) They stumbled at Jesus because they were unable to forsake their dependence on works in favor of faith in Him. (See Romans 9:33; I Peter 2:4-8.) They could not comprehend how one person, Jesus Christ, could achieve for them and on their behalf, by one act on the cross, what they attempted to achieve by a lifetime of striving to adhere to the law of Moses.

Christ: The End of the Law

The Jewish people needed to abandon their fruitless attempts to attain righteousness by the works of the law and to believe on Jesus Christ, whose coming terminated the law: "For Christ is the end of the law for righteousness to everyone who believes" (Romans 10:4). One of the greatest purposes for the law of Moses was to bring Israel to the Messiah.[11] Since that purpose had been accomplished, the only requirement remaining was for the people of Israel to believe on Jesus, to put their complete trust in Him for salvation. To continue to seek righteousness by the works of the law was to stumble.[12]

The Law's Righteousness Is Based on Performance

Romans 10:5 quotes Moses to demonstrate the contrast between the righteousness available on the basis of the law and that available by faith in Christ: "For Moses writes about the righteousness which is of the law, 'The man who does those things shall live by them.'" The righteousness available by the works of the law apart from faith was not soteriological, but relational.[13] It came not merely by believing, but by doing. It was a righteousness that even people who rejected Jesus Christ could attain; it was self-righteousness. (See Philippians 3:6, 9.) The life that resulted from the righteousness of the law was not eternal life, but long life in the land promised to Abraham. This righteousness contrasts sharply with the righteousness of faith. (See Romans 10:6.)

Love Fulfills the Law

Romans 13:1-7 discusses the believer's responsibility to civil government. Romans 13:8 provides a bridge from one's responsibility to civil government to one's responsibility to love his neighbor: "Owe no one anything except to love one another, for he who loves another has fulfilled the law." Contextually, believers are not to withhold their taxes and customs from civil government. The only debt that a believer never fully pays off, the only "debt" upon which he must forever make "payments," is the debt of love.

He is to love others, for "he who loves another has fulfilled the law." The sentiment here is the same as that of Jesus, when He identified the great commandment of the law as the command to love God, and the second to be like it: love your neighbor. (See Matthew 22:37-39.) As Jesus said, "On these two commandments hang all the Law and the Prophets" (Matthew 22:40). The entire Hebrew Scriptures aim at bringing people to a place of loving God and loving others.

Romans 13:9-10 quotes some of the Ten Commandments: "For the commandments, 'You shall not commit adultery,' 'You shall not murder,' 'You shall not steal,' 'You shall not bear false witness,' 'You shall not covet,' and if there is any other commandment, are all summed up in this saying, namely, 'You shall love your neighbor as yourself.' Love does no harm to a neighbor; therefore love is the fulfillment of the law."

The first four of the Ten Commandments given to ancient Israel instructed them in their responsibility to love God. The last six instructed them in their responsibility to love others. (See Exodus 20:1-17.) It is interesting that this passage does not quote all six of the Ten Commandments that have to do with loving others. It quotes five of them (the critical Greek text omits "You shall not bear false witness," in which case the passage quotes only four), and then concludes, "If there is any other commandment."

To Jews who believed the law was still in effect, it would have been unthinkable to deal so casually with the Ten Commandments. With the coming of the new covenant, however, the significance is no longer on precise listings of commandments and prohibitions, but on the essence of the ethical commandments: love. Those who love do not need detailed lists of what they should and should not do; love is its own law, higher even than the 613 commandments of the law of Moses. A person who walks in love will not violate any ethical command included in the law of Moses.

Some have thought that Romans 13:9 indicates the law of Moses is still in effect. But there is no suggestion that these verses reestablish the law of Moses as a code of conduct for believers under the new covenant. (See Romans 3:20-21, 27-28, 31.) Rather, the law of Moses is superseded by the new covenant command to love. (See John 13:34.)

Notes

[1]See discussion under "The Law Established."

[2]The Greek word *paidagogos*, translated "schoolmaster" by the KJV, describes a household slave who was charged with the discipline of the young boys of the family. He was responsible to do everything within his power to preserve the moral purity of his charges.

[3]See page 59, note 15.

[4]Charles C. Ryrie, *The Ryrie Study Bible*, King James Version (Chicago: Moody Press, 1976, 1978), 1773.

[5]J. Dwight Pentecost, "The Purpose of the Law," *The Bib Sac Reader* (n.d.), 107-114.

[6]Robert P. Lightner, "A Dispensational Response to Theonomy," *Bibliotheca Sacra* (July-September 1986), 228-45.

[7]See discussion under "The Law Established."

[8]In I John 1:1-2, in a clear parallel to John 1:1-14, John identifies the "Word" as the "Word of life," declaring that life was manifested and that life was with the Father. The life of God cannot be a separate person from Him.

[9]See discussion under "The Law Gives No Power over Sin."

[10]See discussion under "Advantages of Being Jewish" in chapter 6.

[11]See discussion under "The Law Established" and the opening paragraph of this chapter.

[12]See discussion under "Stumbling at the Stumbling Stone."

[13]See discussion under "The Righteousness of the Law" in chapter 1.

Grace:
Extending the Free Gift of God

The word "grace" is translated from the Greek *charis*, which has to do with a free gift. The word appears in a variety of forms in the literature of the New Testament, but always with the idea of some kind of favor freely given. For example, I Corinthians 12-14 uses a form of the word, *charismata*, to describe the nine gifts of the Holy Spirit.

Grace: More Than Unmerited Favor

In Romans 1:5, Paul wrote, "Through Him we have received grace and apostleship for obedience to the faith among all nations for His name." Paul received grace and the appointment to be an apostle through Jesus Christ. To Paul, the grace of God certainly was the unmerited favor of God graciously extended to man, but it was more than that. The grace of God, by definition a free gift, is a powerful force that works within the believer, giving him right desires and right abilities. (See Romans 3:24; 4:4; 5:15, 17; 11:6; 12:3, 6; I Corinthians 3:10; 15:10; II Corinthians 9:8; 12:9; Galatians 2:21; Hebrews 4:16; Philippians 2:13.)

God graciously gave Paul the desire and the ability to declare the gospel among all nations. This was Paul's "apostleship," or his "sending." The grace and apostleship given to Paul were two completely different things: his apostleship was a gift of the grace of God.

The reference to "all nations" has to do with the Gentiles. To the Jewish people, any reference to the "nations" was a reference to non-Jews; only they were a *chosen* nation (Psalm 33:12; 147:20). The purpose of Paul being sent to the Gentiles was to bring them to "obedience to the faith." Contextually, the faith they were to obey was faith in the gospel and ultimately faith in the One in whom the gospel was personified: Jesus Christ.

The Source of Grace

The conclusion to Paul's lengthy greeting to the church at Rome is virtually identical to that of all his letters: "To all who are in Rome, beloved of God, called to be saints: Grace to you and peace from God our Father and the Lord Jesus Christ" (Romans 1:7). It was standard practice in personal correspondence of the day to wish peace upon one's readers, but Paul included grace. He recognized the source of these blessings as "God our Father and the Lord Jesus Christ."

For a devout Jew like Paul to identify in one breath "the Lord Jesus Christ" with "God our Father" was an undeniable assertion of the deity of Jesus. As strict monotheists, Jews put nothing and no one on the level of God. To identify the Lord Jesus with the Father as the giver of grace and peace means that Jesus is "equal with God." (See John 5:18; Philippians 2:6.) Since Jesus Christ is the brightness of God's glory and the express image of His person (Hebrews 1:3), and since the emphasis of the greeting is on the Incarnation, it is clear that the listing of "God our Father" and "the Lord Jesus Christ" in the same phrase indicates that the incarnate God is equal in every way to God unincarnate. That is, the God we know in the person of Jesus Christ is the same God who was known prior to the Incarnation and is still known by those who have never seen Him in His human existence.

Imparting a Spiritual Gift

Paul wrote, "For I long to see you, that I may impart to you some spiritual gift, so that you may be established" (Romans 1:11). The word translated "gift" is *charisma*, from *charis*. This word does not mean that he sought to give them one of the nine spiritual gifts; the gifts of the Spirit are given only by the Spirit. (See I Corinthians 12:11.) He desired to exercise the spiritual gifts given to him for the benefit of the Romans, to "establish" them. The most effective vehicle of personal ministry is to focus on using the gifts one has received to strengthen and encourage others. (See I Peter 4:10-11; Ephesians 4:11-12; I Corinthians 12:15-28; Romans 12:3-8.)

Justified Freely by His Grace

The next mention of grace occurs in Romans 3:24: "Being justified freely by His grace through the redemption that is in Christ Jesus." This verse clearly identifies justification as a free gift of God. It has nothing to do with merit. The word translated "redemption" means, in its verb form, "to loose" or "to set free." By the free gift of justification, believers are loosed and set free from the penalty of their sins. (See Romans 3:23.) The law of Moses proclaimed the guilt of all (Romans 3:19), but by the grace of God people can be released from that guilt.

Grace or Debt?

After explaining how Abraham was counted righteous on the basis of his faith, not works, Romans 4:4 says, "Now to him who works, the wages are not counted as grace but as debt." The rewards for work done are not free gifts (grace), but wages (debt). Only if salvation is by faith can it be a gift; if it is a reward for works, then it is something God owes us, and rather than glorifying God, we could boast that we have earned our salvation.

Faith and Grace

Since Abraham was counted righteous on the basis of faith, even before he was circumcised, he is the father of all who believe, whether Gentile or Jew. (See Romans 4:9-12.) God ordained this so that the blessing of Abraham would be available to all who believe, not merely to those who had the law of Moses: "Therefore it is of faith that it might be according to grace, so that the promise might be sure to all the seed, not only to those who are of the law, but also to those who are of the faith of Abraham, who is the father of us all" (Romans 4:16). Since the Abrahamic covenant is a faith covenant, not a works covenant, its blessings come by grace, or as a free gift of God. Thus, *all* of Abraham's seed, Jews and Gentiles, will receive the blessing of Abraham, provided they "are of the faith of Abraham, who is the father of us all." (See John 8:39; Galatians 3:13-14.)

Access by Faith into Grace

Through our Lord Jesus Christ, "we have access by faith into this grace in which we stand, and rejoice in hope of the glory of God" (Romans 5:2). Jesus Christ provided, through the Atonement, a way for sinners to enter the presence of the holy God. (See Hebrews 4:16; 10:20.) We obtain access into God's grace by faith, which Romans defines as genuine trust in and reliance upon Jesus Christ and His work on the cross as the sole means of salvation.

Because grace is a free gift, believers are able to "stand" and to "rejoice in hope" of God's glory. If our relationship with God were characterized by performance or merit rather than grace, we would have no ability to stand and no reason to hope, for not only have we all sinned in the past, but we all continue to fall short of the glory of God. (See Romans 3:23.)

Two Heads: Adam and Christ

Romans 5:12-21 explains in a carefully worded argument the negative universal impact of Adam's sin. Then it contrasts the positive universal impact of Christ's righteousness. As pervasive and destructive as Adam's sin was in its effect, the atonement provided by Christ far superseded it, going beyond what was necessary to reverse the effect of Adam's sin.

In Romans 5:15, we begin to see the marked contrast between Adam's representation of the entire human race and Jesus' representation: "But the free gift is not like the offense. For if by the one man's offense many died, much more the grace of God and the gift by the grace of the one Man, Jesus Christ, abounded to many." The free gift is unlike the offense in that the offense produced death—separation from fellowship with God, while the free gift produced life—restoration to fellowship with God. (See Romans 5:16.)

First-century readers would have understood the "many" to mean the entire human race. In the Greek the definite article is present (*hoi polloi*), indicating not just "many," as in a large number, but "*the* many," as in all humanity.

The repeated use of "much more" underscores the superiority of Christ's atonement over Adam's sin. (See also Romans 5:17, 20.) Though there is a *contrast* between the way Adam and Christ represented the entire human race, there is in a sense no *comparison*, for the righteousness of Jesus far surpassed the sin of Adam.

The work of Jesus Christ results in a "free gift" and "the gift by . . . grace." This concept is important, especially in view of the tendency of Jewish readers to boast in their works as if by their performance they merited salvation. (See Romans 2:17; 3:27.) By definition, anything resulting from grace is free.

The statement that the free gift "abounded to [the] many" does not mean that as a result of Christ's death on the cross all people are automatically saved. This carefully worded argument says that "by the one man's offense [the] many died," indicating the universal spiritual death resulting from Adam's sin, but it avoids saying that by the grace of Jesus Christ [the] many live. It says, "The grace

of the one Man, Jesus Christ, *abounded* to [the] many."
That it, it was done for the many, and it is offered to the
many, but it still must be received in order to be effective
for any individual (verse 17).

We see a further contrast between the effects of
Adam's sin and Christ's righteousness in Romans 5:16:
"And the gift is not like that which came through the one
who sinned. For the judgment which came from one
offense resulted in condemnation, but the free gift which
came from many offenses resulted in justification." The
sin of Adam's produced condemnation and spiritual
death. The free gift offered by Jesus is justification (right
standing with God) and spiritual life. The sin of Adam
resulted in universal death, but the free gift of Jesus gathered up "many offenses" (all the sins ever committed by
the human race) and made atonement for them.

Christ's righteousness overwhelms the effect of
Adam's sin: "For if by the one man's offense death
reigned through the one, much more those who receive
abundance of grace and of the gift of righteousness will
reign in life through the One, Jesus Christ" (Romans
5:17). Adam's sin resulted in death (spiritual separation
from God) reigning universally. But Romans does not say
that as a consequence of Christ's work on the cross life
(spiritual fellowship with God) now reigns universally.
Instead, those who will "reign in life" are those who
"*receive* abundance of grace and of the gift of righteousness." We receive spiritual life by faith in Jesus Christ.
(See John 1:12; Romans 3:22, 26, 30; 4:11-12, 16, 24;
5:1-2.)

The phrase "much more" demonstrates the superiority of Christ's work over Adam's sin. (See Romans 5:15,

20.) The grace (free gift) received by believers is *abundant*; it is more than necessary to achieve the desired result.

Righteousness (right standing with God) is a free gift extended to those who "receive abundance of grace." The Roman letter emphasizes that a person does not earn favor with God by his performance but receives it as a free gift by relying exclusively on Jesus Christ for salvation.

Romans 5:20-21 explains the purpose for the law of Moses: "Moreover the law entered that the offense might abound. But where sin abounded, grace abounded much more, so that as sin reigned in death, even so grace might reign through righteousness to eternal life through Jesus Christ our Lord." The law made it exceedingly clear that people were sinners. But grace overwhelms condemnation so that the reign of grace in eternal life consumes the reign of sin in death for those who relate to God on the basis of the righteousness of Jesus Christ rather than the works of the law.

An Improper Question

In a question reminiscent of those in Romans 3:5-8, Romans 6:1 asks, "What shall we say then? Shall we continue in sin that grace may abound?" As in Romans 3:5, this passage speaks from the perspective of human wisdom in order to dramatically communicate its point to spiritually immature readers. (See Romans 6:19.) Since grace overwhelms sin (Romans 5:20), it may seem reasonable from a human standpoint to encourage people to sin all the more so grace could be even more abundant. But any readers who think this misses the point.

As this chapter develops, the reason for the abundance of grace is not to doom people to slavery to sin so that the grace of God will stand out in even more bold relief against the sordid backdrop of sin. The reason for the abundance of grace is to release people from slavery to sin. Grace abounds not merely to demonstrate the depravity of sin, but to assure that no matter how deep one may be in the pit of sin, grace can reach farther down.

Under Grace, Not under Law

"For sin shall not have dominion over you, for you are not under law but under grace. What then? Shall we sin because we are not under law but under grace? Certainly not!" (Romans 6:14-15). To be "under law" means to be under obligation to the law of Moses as a way of life.[1] To be "under grace" means to be under grace as a way of life. Sin rules those who are obligated to the law, for the law stirs up the sinful passions of sin. (See Romans 7:5.) Although grace does not eliminate the sin nature in those who are regenerate, it suppresses it and gives power over it. Emphasizing law stirs the rebellion of the sin nature. But emphasizing the believer's acceptance to God on the basis of His grace helps release him from the compulsion to sin and stirs within him the desire to please God. Through the power of the Holy Spirit he has both the desire and power to do God's will. (See Philippians 2:13.)

The Election of Grace

A major portion—three entire chapters—of Paul's letter to the believers in Rome is taken up with an examination of national Israel's past, present, and future. As it fits in the overall flow of the letter, this discussion was no doubt made necessary by the repeated assertions that the law of Moses has terminated (Romans 3:20-22, 27-28; 7:4-6; 8:3) and that ethnic Jewishness does not provide salvation (Romans 2:11-13, 17-29; 3:9-19, 29-30; 4:9-15; 5:20; 7:5, 8, 10-11, 14). At this point in the letter, first-century Jewish readers probably were asking themselves if the heritage they had long valued was of any real significance.

On the other hand, first-century Gentile readers may have been strengthened in their libertarian boasting (Romans 11:17-24) by the rebuke of their Jewish brethren's sense of moral superiority (Romans 2:1-24; 3:9-19).

Chapters 9-11 serve to restore the sense of destiny national Israel had deservedly held for many centuries. Although national Israel, who had been elected by God, was now under His divine disapproval, their future restoration in His eyes was assured. But those from among national Israel who believed in Christ were already included in an election based on the grace of God: "Even so then, at this present time there is a remnant according to the election of grace. And if by grace, then it is no longer of works; otherwise grace is no longer grace. But if it is of works, it is no longer grace; otherwise work is no longer work" (Romans 11:5-6).

Just as there were seven thousand faithful Israelites in the days of Elijah (Romans 11:2-4), so there is a remnant even now, at the time of the nation's rejection of the Messiah and of their consequent rejection by God. These Jewish believers are the remnant "according to the election of grace." That is, they are included in the remnant because they have responded to the grace of God in faith.

It is impossible to mix grace and works in an attempt to relate to God. Grace excludes works; works exclude grace. The Jewish remnant did not attain that status by their own self-reliant efforts. They did not earn or merit this status. Since their faith response to God was made possible by the grace of God, their response could not be called "works."

In the Book of Romans, things done by one's own strength in attempt to gain favor with God are "works." Things done by the enablement of the Holy Spirit are not. The source of desire and ability to do things that glorify and please God is not one's own strength; it is the grace of God. The reason grace and works cannot be mixed is because they represent two radically different approaches to God. The works approach calls attention to one's own achievements in an attempt to gain favor with God. The grace approach appeals exclusively to the work of Christ on the cross for right standing with God. One is an approach of pride; the other of humility.

Seven Gifts of Grace

Romans 12:3-8 encourages the readers to discover their spiritual gifts and to minister according to their unique spiritual giftedness: "For I say, through the grace given to me, to everyone who is among you, not to think of himself more highly than he ought to think, but to think soberly, as God has dealt to each one a measure of faith. For as we have many members in one body, but all the members do not have the same function, so we, being many, are one body in Christ, and individually members of one another. Having then gifts differing according to the grace that is given to us, let us use them: if prophecy, let us prophesy in proportion to our faith; or ministry, let us use it in our ministering; he who teaches, in teaching; he who exhorts, in exhortation; he who gives, with liberality; he who leads, with diligence; he who shows mercy, with cheerfulness."

Paul credited all he did to the grace of God. (See I Corinthians 15:10.) His words did not spring from his own musings, but from the influence of God's grace upon him. Specifically, Paul's "grace" ("free gift") was his apostleship. (See Romans 1:5; 15:15-16.) As an apostle of God, he commanded the Romans to not think of themselves more highly than they should, but to think soberly, "as God has dealt to each one a measure of faith."

The word translated "soberly" means to be in one's right mind. God has given each person "a measure of faith," and it is according to this faith that one must think. There is no idea here that a believer must belittle or degrade himself. The idea is that each believer must carefully evaluate his own giftedness by means of the faith freely given by God.

This is not a call to "visualization" or "positive thinking" or goal setting. It is instead a call to sober reflection and assessment of the gifts and abilities one possesses by the grace of God. Faith is essentially trust, and one can evaluate his giftedness by determining in which of the seven areas of service he is able to trust God for direction and productivity.

Apparently there were some Roman Christians who did think of themselves more highly than they ought, and the command here is intended as a corrective. No doubt some were attempting to minister outside of their gifts, and some who may have been ministering according to their gifts were exceeding God's leading.

In words similar to those of I Corinthians 12:12-17 and Ephesians 4:15-16, Romans 12 compares the church to a human body. Just as the various members of the human body do not have the same functions, so the members of the body of Christ (the church, Colossians 1:18) have differing functions. Not only are believers, in spite of the diversity of their gifts, "one body in Christ," they are also "members of one another." That is, they are connected inseparably to one another in function and service, just as are the members of the human body. Here, the letter emphasized to a church composed of two somewhat divided factions, Jewish and Gentile, their inseparable oneness in Christ. They needed to lay aside the issues that divided them in favor of the more important issue that united them: their identification with Jesus Christ.

The various gifts given to the individual members of the body of Christ are "grace" gifts. That is, they are freely given. There is no thought of gifts being given as rewards or on the basis of merit or performance. Both the words "gifts" (*charismata*) and "grace" (*charin*) spring from the same root word, *charis*. By definition, a gift is free. (See Matthew 10:8.) As they are received freely, they are to be ministered freely. (See I Peter 4:10-11.)

Although the same word, *charismata*, appears here and in I Corinthians 12-14 (dealing with spiritual gifts), these gifts seem to be of a different nature. The only common ground with the nine spiritual gifts of I Corinthians 12:8-10 is prophecy, and the only common ground with the positional gifts of Ephesians 4:11 is teaching and prophecy. But it is not clear that the gift of "teaching" in

Romans 12:7 makes the person a "teacher" in the sense of Ephesians 4:11, or that a person with the gift of "prophecy" is a "prophet" in the sense of Ephesians 4:11.

The gifts of I Corinthians 12-14 are "sign" gifts for the edification of the church (I Corinthians 14:3-5, 12; see also Mark 16:17, 20). The gifts of Ephesians 4:11-12 are actually individuals God has specially prepared and given to the church to equip the saints. We can call the gifts in Romans 12 "motivational gifts," for they seem to describe the motivating influences upon individual members of the body of Christ for Christian service.

Thus, a person may be a pastor (Ephesians 4:11), but his dominant motivational gift may be teaching, whereas another member of the body of Christ may not fill any role described in Ephesians 4:11 but may still have the gift of teaching. The possible combinations of positional gifts, motivational gifts, and spiritual gifts are so numerous that they provide an enormous amount of variety in the body of Christ.

The first of the seven gifts here is prophecy, which I Corinthians 12:10 also mentions. Perhaps it is mentioned first because of its importance. (See I Corinthians 14:1.) Prophecy edifies (strengthens and builds up), exhorts (encourages), and comforts (I Corinthians 14:3). It seems certain that a prophet will have the gift of prophecy (I Corinthians 14:29-32), but it does not follow that everyone who exercises the gift of prophecy fills the office of a prophet. (See I Corinthians 11:5; 13:2, 8-9; 14:1, 3-5, 22, 24, 31.) I Corinthians 14:1 urges every believer to seek to prophesy, but surely it does not urge everyone to seek the office of a prophet.

To prophesy is to speak on behalf of God. Words from

God, even though spoken through human beings, have amazing power to strengthen the weak, encourage the discouraged, and comfort the troubled.

How can a person know if he has the gift of prophecy? There seem to be three major keys to identifying the spiritual gift or gifts God has given a person. They are: (1) desire; (2) ability; (3) confirmation. (See Philippians 2:13; II Timothy 1:6, 18.)

First, it is God who works in us to give us right desires ("to will"). Second, God works in us to give us the ability ("to do") what He gives us the desire to do. God will never give us the desire to do something that He refuses to give us the ability to do. Therefore, a specific desire relative to the spiritual gifts may be a desire from God. And if He gives the desire for a certain gift or gifts, he will surely give the ability to minister these gifts.

We are to "covet earnestly the best gifts" and to "desire spiritual gifts" (I Corinthians 12:31; 14:1). There is nothing evil or wrong about desiring spiritual gifts. Indeed, the desire is from God, and it is supported by His Word.

The third key is confirmation. If God has truly given a person a spiritual gift, he will not be the only one who knows it. The church will bear witness to it. Others will recognize the operation of the gifts to be genuine. In Timothy's case, the gift God gave him was confirmed by the laying on of Paul's hands and by prophecy.

A person to whom God has given the gift of prophecy will have a desire to speak words that strengthen, encourage, and comfort others. Of course, to a certain extent, everyone in the body of Christ can and should have such a desire. All seven of the gifts mentioned here have characteristics that may be in the lives of all believers. Nevertheless, this passage declares that each believer has received a specific gift.

Practical experience suggests that each believer will tend to have a dominant gift and one or more secondary gifts. For instance, a person may have prophecy as the dominant gift and teaching as a secondary gift. In this case, his greatest desire and ability will be to prophesy, but to a lesser extent he will also desire and be able to teach.

The person who has the gift of prophecy will be alert for opportunities to speak words that strengthen, encourage, and comfort others. This may be in a private or corporate setting. Perhaps these words can come by other means than by speaking. For example, some people may be gifted at writing words—whether in personal correspondence or for wider circulation—that perform the functions of prophecy.

The King James Version translates the last phrase of Romans 12:6 as "let us prophesy according to the proportion of faith," while the New King James Version translates it as "let us prophesy in proportion to our faith." A literal translation of the Greek words *kata ten analogian tes pisteos* is "according to the agreement to the faith." The word translated "proportion" (*analogian*) is transliterated into English as "analogy." The point is that all prophecy must agree with the truth already revealed in the Scriptures. (See Jude 3; I Corinthians 14:29; I Thessalonians 5:19-21.) No spiritual gift, including prophecy, is valid if it conflicts with Scripture. Scripture is the final authority.

The gift of "ministry" has to do with serving. *Diakon-*

ian, translated "ministry," comes from a root word meaning "to serve." Acts 6:1-7 records an example of believers who were especially gifted in this area. The church selected seven men to serve (*diakonein*) tables. We see the wisdom of placing believers in the specific area of their giftedness in that following the appointment of these seven servers, "the word of God spread, and the number of the disciples multiplied greatly in Jerusalem" (Acts 6:7).

Though all believers are to serve others (Galatians 5:13), some are specially gifted and fulfilled in serving roles. As in Acts 6, it may be something as practical as serving food in a kitchen, but it will in all cases result in relieving those who are gifted in other areas to function in the area of their giftedness. As the apostles noted in Acts 6:2, it is not reasonable for people to abandon the area of their giftedness to function in an area for which they are not gifted. This does not mean it is beneath anyone's dignity, including apostles, to function in any of the seven areas Romans 12 describes. It simply means that every person has a particular place in the body of Christ for which he is uniquely suited, a place where he will be most effective and fulfilled.

The person who has the gift of teaching should focus on developing and using that gift to the best of his ability. This person may not fill the office of a teacher as described in I Corinthians 12:28 and Ephesians 4:11, but there are many opportunities for teaching other than in a formal sense or before large groups of people. For example, Paul instructed Titus to direct "the older women" to be "teachers of good things," including admonishing "the young women to love their husbands, to love their children, to be discreet, chaste, homemakers, good, obedient to their own husbands, that the word of God may not be blasphemed" (Titus 2:3-5). Paul told Timothy to commit to faithful men the things he had heard from Paul so those faithful men "will be able to teach others also" (II Timothy 2:2).

A person who has the gift of teaching will be interested in explaining theoretical or practical truths to others. He will enjoy the detail work of researching, synthesizing, and creating learning materials and environments. He tends to be very concerned about determining the right meaning of words and phrases, especially biblical texts. As with the gift of prophecy, the person with the gift of teaching may exercise it in addition to or apart from lecturing or public speaking. He may teach by writing or other forms of communication.

Some believers are gifted to exhort, or encourage, others. Though this gift may bear some similarity to the gift of prophecy, the gift of exhortation focuses on only one aspect of the function of prophecy. Specifically, prophecy serves to strengthen, encourage, and comfort, but the person with the gift of exhortation is most intensely interested in encouragement. Perhaps surprisingly, he may not be as interested or as capable in comforting and strengthening the weak. He will tend to focus on trying to cheer people up. Sometimes, however, hurting people do not need good cheer; they need empathy. (See Romans 12:15.) In these cases, attempts to encourage usually result in further discouragement or even depression and feelings of hopelessness.

The person who is gifted to give should do so with "liberality." (See II Corinthians 8:2; 9:11, 13.) All believers are, of course, to give. (See II Corinthians 9:6-15.)

But some have a special ability to give and receive special joy from finding opportunities to share with others in their needs. These people are often quiet, unobtrusive, and behind the scenes. Those who wish to make a great public display of their giving probably do not possess this gift; instead, they probably are giving reluctantly in order to be seen of others. (See Matthew 6:1-4.)

The gift of leading has to do with administration. The word translated "rule" or "lead" is *proistamenos*, which literally means "standing before." Those whose gift is to "stand in front" of others are to do so diligently. This gift is not necessarily restricted to teachers or pastors, but it includes those who are responsible for planning, organizing, and administering. In many cases, of course, those who fulfill the positional gifts of Ephesians 4:11 will also possess the gift of administration.

The person who has the gift of administration will tend to enjoy planning and working with details. He can break down a long-range goal into the steps it takes to reach that goal. He enjoys challenges and organizing people, tasks, and resources. This person may sometimes grow frustrated with those who thwart his efforts by not following his plans, and he may consider getting outside the area of his giftedness in an attempt to rebuke or correct them. But he is at his best when he faithfully continues to do what he is gifted to do, even though people are not perfect and will sometimes make his task difficult.

The person who is gifted to show mercy will be sensitive to the needs of other people. By contrast, the person with the gift of administration may be so caught up in the details of planning and setting goals that he may not be aware of the hurts and suffering of people around him.

His eyes are on the future and what is to be done; he may grow impatient dealing with present problems, especially if he perceives them to be a consequence of human weakness. But to the person whose gift is to show mercy, the wounds of others are obvious. This person looks for opportunities to empathize with others.

Since there is always the temptation for the giver of mercy to identify so completely with those who are suffering that their sadness is transferred to him, verse 8 reminds those who have this gift to show mercy "with cheerfulness," or gladly. The person who shows mercy may be tempted to be judgmental of those who do not have this gift; he cannot understand why everyone is not as aware of the needs of hurting people as he is. But he is not to be detoured from his mission by the insensitivity of others; he is to focus on ministering out of his gift.

The person with the gift of showing mercy will tend to have the patience to listen to people's problems, even when they need help repeatedly. He enjoys visiting the sick and hurting, and he is reluctant to pronounce the judgment of God on anyone.

In order for the body of Christ to be whole and to have the balance needed, it must have the variety of motivational gifts listed here. Someone must speak on behalf of God; someone must serve in practical ways; someone must teach; someone must encourage; someone must give; someone must provide administration; someone must show mercy on those who are suffering.

A Boldly Written Letter

As he moved toward the conclusion of his letter to the church in Rome, Paul wrote, "Nevertheless, brethren, I have written more boldly to you on some points, as reminding you, because of the grace given to me by God" (Romans 15:15).

In spite of his recognition of the fullness of goodness and knowledge possessed by the Roman believers (Romans 15:14), Paul wrote boldly to remind them of things they needed to know and do. Peter and Jude exercised a similar mission. (See II Peter 1:12; 3:1-2; Jude 3.)

As an example, Christian unity should characterize all believers everywhere. Since this was lacking or damaged in Rome, Paul boldly addressed the issue of unity between Jewish and Gentile believers. (See Romans 2:1, 14-15, 17, 26-27; 3:1, 27, 29-30; 4:9-12; 9:30-33; 10:11-13, 19-21; 11:1, 11-25; 12:4-5, 9, 16; 14:1-7, 10, 14-17; 15:5-12.)

The "grace," or gift, to which Paul referred is his apostleship, specifically to the Gentiles. (See Romans 1:5; 12:3.) Because of the gift of God's grace, Paul had the necessary authority to address the issues he dealt with in this letter to the Roman believers.

Grace Be with You

In two verses near the end of his letter, Paul expressed his hope that the grace of God would be with his readers: "And the God of peace will crush Satan under your feet shortly. The grace of our Lord Jesus Christ be with you. Amen. . . . The grace of our Lord Jesus Christ be with you all. Amen" (Romans 16:20, 24).

In a metaphor reflecting Genesis 3:15, this passage assures believers that God will shortly crush Satan under their feet. Like Romans 15:13, it identifies God as the "God of peace." Satan had attempted to damage the church in Rome by causing "divisions and offenses," by promoting ethnic division, and by sending persecution. But this would soon come to an end.

In this benediction, Paul wished for the grace of the Lord Jesus Christ to be with the Roman believers. In view of all he could have wished for them, this choice is significant. He opened the letter by wishing grace and peace upon his readers (Romans 1:7), and he closed it by expressing his desire that grace would be with them. These are not mere words. Grace, the free gift of the favor of God and of right desires and abilities, is indispensable to the Christian life.

Romans 15:24 repeats a portion of Romans 15:20. Since verse 24 is missing from several Greek manuscripts, many scholars consider it not to be original but a scribal reproduction of verse 20. In any case, the words themselves are inspired of God and accurately reflect Paul's abiding concern that his readers be the recipients of the grace of God.

Note
[1]See discussion under "Not Under Law" in chapter 2.

Faith:
Trusting God to Be God

Some thirty-nine times the Book of Romans uses the Greek *pistis*. In the KJV, the word is translated "faith" and "believeth." Another twenty-one times, Romans uses *pisteuo*, which is derived from *pistis* and which is translated "believeth," "believe," "believed," and "believing." Once, it is translated "committed." In Romans 3:3, *apisteo* appears, translated "did not believe."

About sixty times, then, in sixteen chapters, Romans refers to faith or the lack of faith. Such a frequent use of the term means it is a major theme in the letter.

To understand the emphasis of Romans correctly, it is essential to grasp the significance of these words, especially since so many people misunderstand the meaning of faith. Some have confused faith with a way of thinking, a mental attitude one can adopt at will. There is a tendency to equate faith with positive thinking or a positive mental attitude. Some have gone so far as to suggest that faith is the exercise of one's powers of imagination in visualizing what one desires until it comes into reality. Faith thus becomes mental imagery, and the more vivid the mental image the more powerful the faith. In a negative sense, some think that it is faith to deny sickness, illness, or pain. All of these ideas are far from biblical faith.

The Bible knows nothing of "faith" that exists in the realm of the mind alone. Faith is not mere mental assent to a set of facts. Nor is it denying reality and creating one's own world by mental gymnastics. Though, in some cases—especially when it appears with the definite article—faith has to do with the facts of doctrinal truth (Jude 3; Romans 1:5; Galatians 1:23; I Timothy 4:1, 6), biblical faith ordinarily describes *trust in God.* It is not incorrect to translate *pisteuo* or *pistis* as "believe" or "faith" or "confidence," as long as we realize that to believe or to have faith or to have confidence in biblical terms means to trust in God. The adjective *pistos* means to be faithful in the sense of being trustworthy and dependable. Faith views God as being worthy of one's trust.

Thus, biblical faith has nothing to do with attempting to manipulate circumstances to suit one's fancy. It has to do with trusting in God regardless of the circumstances. This is nowhere better illustrated than in Job's stirring declaration, in the midst of the most devastating trial, "Though He slay me, yet will I trust Him" (Job 13:15).

It is true that faith in God will often result in pleasant blessings—healing, the supply of needs, prayer answered as one hoped it would be (Hebrews 11:32-35). It is equally true that faith in God sometimes results in painful circumstances—torture, trials, and even death (Hebrews 11:35-

39). In the final analysis, the prayer of faith is the prayer that submits to the will of God. (See I John 5:14-15.) Faith is not twisting God's arm; it is trusting God's arms.

The factor most commonly leading to a perversion of the idea of faith is a misunderstanding of the connection between faith and the working of miracles or answered prayer as described by Jesus in the Gospels (Matthew 9:28-29; 15:28; 17:20-21) and by others elsewhere (Acts 14:9; I Corinthians 12:9; 13:2). By looking only at a narrow range of biblical evidence, some have concluded that faith is some kind of "force" which causes things to happen. Tying closely together the supposed power of spoken words with mental imagery, some have suggested that words are "containers" that, when filled with the "force" of faith, obligate God to perform at our behest. In other words, by speaking the "word of faith," we can enact some kind of "spiritual laws" that assure results as certainly as "natural laws."

One of the main passages these teachers rely upon for this view of faith is Mark 11:20-24. After Jesus' disciples observed the withered fig tree, He said to them, "Have faith in God. For assuredly, I say to you, whoever says to this mountain, 'Be removed and be cast into the sea,' and does not doubt in his heart, but believes that those things he says will come to pass, he will have whatever he says. Therefore I say to you, whatever things you ask when you pray, believe that you receive them, and you will have them."

The misunderstanding of this text to mean that anything we can imagine will be done if we can visualize it vividly enough begins by ignoring or perverting the clear command: "Have faith in God." Some have suggested that we should translate this command as, "Have the faith of God," but there is absolutely no textual warrant for such a translation.

The actual Greek text reads *echete pistin theou.* *Echete* is an imperative, a command, in the second person plural. It means "you (plural) have." It is a command by Jesus for His disciples to have faith. *Pistin* is the accusative form of *pistis*, which means "faith." The word is not preceded by the definite article; thus to translate it as "the faith" is wrong. *Theou*, from *theos* ("God"), is in the genitive case, which is essentially the case of description.

Some teachers apparently think of every genitive in terms of possession and suppose a genitive must always be translated "of." Therefore, they suggest that *theou* should be translated "of God." From there, it is a short distance to adding the definite article to "faith," and the result is, "Have the faith of God." But, as with any other case in the Greek language, the genitive has a wide variety of uses depending upon construction and context. Here, we have either an objective genitive or a genitive of reference. With an objective genitive, "the genitive *receives* the action, being thus related *as object* to the verbal idea contained in the noun modified."[1] In this case, God is the object of the faith. A genitive of reference qualifies nouns or adjectives. We could understand the sense by the translation "with reference to."[2] In other words, the phrase could be translated, "Have faith with reference to God." Grammatically, we can understand the genitive in this verse either way. That is why reputable translations render the phrase, "Have faith in God."

This phrase is key to understanding the passage. It means our faith, or our trust, must be *in* God. That is, He must be the *object* of our faith. Faith is not a force in itself. The only thing that validates faith is its object. If it is not trust in God, "faith" is merely an exercise in mental manipulation.

The marvelous promise of Jesus that believers can move mountains depends completely on one's prior faith in God. The contextual emphasis of the passage is not on *speaking* to the mountain, or having whatever one *says*, or even on *believing* for answered prayer. The emphasis is on having faith in God. All of these other things are simply the natural by-products of faith, or trust, in God. In other words, *as our trust is in God* we can speak to mountains and believe for answered prayer. And if our trust is in God, we will know to which mountains He wants us to speak, and the things for which He wants us to believe, and the petitions for which we should pray.

The second mistake of those who misinterpret this passage is ignoring the wider testimony of Scripture about answered prayer. John wrote, "Now this is the confidence that we have in Him, that if we ask anything according to His will, He hears us. And if we know that He hears us, whatever we ask, we know that we have the petitions that we have asked of Him" (I John 5:14-15). The assurance that we have our petitions comes from the knowledge that God has heard our prayer. And the knowledge that He has heard our prayer comes from asking *according to His will*. The only prayers we can be certain God will answer according to our desire are those in accordance with His will.

Thus Mark 11:22-24 cannot mean that we set the agenda, and God is forced to do whatever we *say*, so long as we do not doubt. It means that if our trust is in God, and His will is our will, we will speak to the mountains He intends to move, we will have absolute confidence that what we have said will be done—because we know it is

God's will—and we will pray with the confidence that we will receive, for our prayer has been in accordance with the will of God.

The only thing Jesus said would invalidate the promise of Mark 11:23-24 is doubt in one's heart. And the only way to remove doubt completely is to place one's trust exclusively in God. Otherwise, no matter how desperately we wish for a certain thing to come to pass, and no matter how vividly we may imagine it actually transpiring, there is always at least a little question as to whether what we want is what God wants.

Nowhere did Jesus more perfectly demonstrate the prayer of faith than in the Garden of Gethsemane: "O My Father, if it is possible, let this cup pass from Me; nevertheless, not as I will, but as You will" (Matthew 26:39). According to the view of some, if Jesus had been positive enough in His confession, and if He had prayed with enough faith, He could have forced God to arrange another plan for redemption. Jesus did sincerely pray, "If it is possible, let this cup pass from Me." Some have the idea that where there is faith, anything is possible. But some things are simply not possible, because they are not the will of God. It was not possible that Jesus avoid the bitter cup. But His prayer was a demonstration of genuine faith, or trust, in God, for He prayed, "Not as I will, but as You will."

Throughout His life on earth, Jesus never failed in ministry, for He attempted nothing but what was the will of God. (See John 5:19-20.) The success of His ministry was not merely due to His using certain formulas or speaking with great assurance or His putting all doubt out of His heart. Rather His ministry was successful because He was perfectly led by the Spirit and He was completely surrendered to the will of God. (See Matthew 4:1; Luke 4:1, 14, 18; Hebrews 10:7.)

Mark 11:22-24 does not give us a "faith formula" by which we can make anything happen that we can imagine. Instead, it flows with the broad teaching of Scripture on this subject: Where there is genuine trust in God, prayer will be made in accordance with the will of God, and those prayers will be answered.

The suggestion that we must have "the faith of God" or, as some propose, "the God kind of faith," implies that God has faith, and that He does what He does by faith. From this idea, the teaching follows that, since we have faith, we can—like God—create "worlds" of some kind. But God does not need faith; He is God. If He had faith, there would have to be an object of His faith, and that object would be greater than Him. It is we, not God, who need faith, and for our faith to be valid, it must have God as its object.

The most frequent meaning of "faith" in Romans is trust in God. In a few instances, there are other grammatical and contextual uses of the word.

Faith As Doctrine

The first mention of faith in this letter is in Romans 1:5: "Through whom we have received grace and apostleship for obedience to the faith among all nations for His name." God's purpose in sending Paul to the Gentiles was to bring them to "obedience to the faith." The faith—in this case a system of teaching—they were to obey was the gospel of Christ. (See Romans 1:16.)

Faith is not mere mental assent; it includes obedience. It is not simply intellectual agreement with a specific set of facts. *The* faith, another term for "the gospel," requires obedience. (See II Thessalonians 1:8.) Biblical faith always produces behavioral results. (See James 2:14-26.)

Faith's Companions: Hope and Love

There are three qualities by which Paul assessed the relative maturity and spirituality of the churches to which he wrote: faith, hope, and love. In general, Paul commended each church in the early verses of his letters for one or more of these qualities. If any one of the three is missing in his commendation, it seems the letter was written to deal with the quality or qualities in which the church was deficient.

In Romans 1:8, Paul commended the church at Rome for its faith, which was so well known as to be the topic of discussion among believers everywhere: "First, I thank my God through Jesus Christ for you all, that your faith is spoken of throughout the whole world." Again in Romans 1:12, Paul commended the Romans for this quality. Although the letter mentions hope ten times, in no case did Paul commend the church at Rome for its hope. Instead, he prayed that they would abound in hope (Romans 15:13). The letter mentions love eleven times, but as with hope, there is no commendation for the Romans' love. There are, however, repeated encouragements to love (Romans 8:28; 12:9-10; 13:8-10).

The church at Corinth was a carnal church (I Corinthians 3:1), and Paul did not commend them for faith, hope, or love. Instead, he identified all three qualities as suitable goals for the Corinthians (I Corinthians 13:13). The church at Corinth apparently matured in the quality of faith by the time Paul wrote his second letter to them (II Corinthians 1:24; 10:15). They still seemed, however, to be deficient in hope and love. It was apparently reported that they had matured in love, but Paul asked them to prove their love (II Corinthians 8:7-8, 24).

The churches of Galatia were being swayed from their exclusive faith in Christ to a form of Judaism (Galatians 1:6-9). It is no surprise, then, that Paul did not commend them for faith, hope, or love. Instead, he encouraged them to develop these qualities. We see his encouragement to develop faith in Galatians 3:2, 5, 7-9, 11, 14, 23-26; 5:5-6, 22. Encouragement to develop hope occurs in Galatians 5:5, while encouragement to develop love is in Galatians 5:6, 13-14, 22.

The church in Ephesus was a relatively mature church, and Paul commended the believers there for their faith and love (Ephesians 1:15). They were apparently deficient in hope, and Paul prayed that they would grow in that area (Ephesians 1:18). Revelation 2:4 discloses, however, that by the time John wrote the final book in the New Testament, the Ephesian church had turned away from the love they formerly had.

Paul commended the Philippians for their faith (Philippians 1:25; 2:17) and prayed that their love would abound more (Philippians 1:9). Though they apparently had a measure of love, it needed development and maturing (Philippians 2:2). He did not commend them for their hope.

Paul commended the Colossians for their faith, hope, and love (Colossians 1:4-5). The essential message of the book is that the believers should stand fast in their relationships with Jesus Christ and not be moved by legalists, mystics, or ascetics.

One of the most interesting examples of the way in which faith, hope, and love are yardsticks to measure the maturity and spiritual well-being of a church is in the letters to the Thessalonians. The first letter commends the believers for their faith, hope, and love (I Thessalonians 1:3). But after the first letter, some false teacher had apparently forged a letter under Paul's name to the Thessalonians claiming that the Day of Christ had already come (II Thessalonians 2:1-2). This false teaching robbed the Thessalonians of their hope, so that Paul could commend them only for their faith and love (II Thessalonians 1:3). Clearly, Paul wrote his second letter to restore hope to the Thessalonians (II Thessalonians 2:3-17).

Like most of the first-century churches, the church at Rome needed to mature in certain areas. Specifically, the believers in Rome were apparently deficient in hope and love.

The common pattern in Paul's letters to churches was to commend them in the early verses for their strengths, then to correct in the main body of the letter their deficiencies or excesses, and finally to commend them again in the closing for their strengths. The final commendation to the Romans comes in 16:19.

This approach has been called the "plus-minus-plus" or "positive-negative-positive" technique. When it is necessary to offer correction, it is wise first to commend and then to reinforce the commendation after giving the correction. This principle is useful in all relationships, including the parent-child relationship. It is wise for spiritual leaders to use this approach in preaching, teaching, and counseling.

Mutual Faith

Paul realized that his ministry to the Romans would not be a one-way street. After explaining why he wanted to visit them, he added, "That is, that I may be encouraged together with you by the mutual faith both of you and me" (Romans 1:12). They too had faith, they had spiritual gifts (see Romans 1:11), and they would minister to Paul, encouraging him. Those who are called into positional ministries must realize that all of God's people have spiritual gifts, and when they are released to exercise their gifts, much good results.

The Just Shall Live by Faith

Romans 1:16-17 is a dramatic statement that forms the theme of the letter: "For I am not ashamed of the gospel of Christ, for it is the power of God to salvation for everyone who believes, for the Jew first and also for the Greek. For in it the righteousness of God is revealed from faith to faith; as it is written, 'The just shall live by faith.'"

By the miracle of regeneration Paul had changed from a hater and a persecutor of the church to a bold proclaimer and defender of the gospel. (See Acts 22:4; 26:11; I Corinthians 15:9; Galatians 1:13, 23.)

The good news (Greek, *euangelion*, "gospel") is God's power that results in salvation for all who believe it. It is the good news of Christ, which means it has to do with the identity and work of Jesus Christ. Concerning His identity, He is the Son of God, and thus divine (Romans 1:3, 4). Concerning His work, He dealt with the sin problem completely and universally in the Atonement. Because of the coming of Christ, there is no reason for anyone to be lost. This is indeed good news.

The word "salvation" is a broad term, including past, present, and future aspects. (See Luke 7:50; Romans 5:10; 6:14; 8:2, 18-23; 13:11; I Corinthians 1:18; 3:15; 5:5;

15:42-44; II Corinthians 2:15; 3:18; Galatians 2:19-20; Ephesians 2:5, 8; Philippians 1:19; 2:12-13; II Thessalonians 2:13; II Timothy 1:9; Hebrews 10:36; I Peter 1:5; I John 3:2.) There is no consequence of sin—past, present, or future—that the blood of Jesus does not resolve.

Salvation is not available only to a limited number of people. There is no idea here of a limited atonement or that the only people who can be saved are those who have been individually predestined or elected by a sovereign act of God at some point in the distant past. The only condition Scripture imposes here is that one must believe.

Salvation by faith does not mean that the only thing involved in receiving the gift of salvation is to assent mentally to the historical facts about Jesus' person and work. Multitudes believe academically in Jesus as the incarnation of God and in His death on the cross as the atonement for sins, but they have never been saved, for they have never placed their faith (trust) in Him for salvation nor obeyed the gospel. (See II Thessalonians 1:8.)

The normative expression of genuine faith throughout the New Testament is first to repent from sins (Luke 13:3, 5; 24:47; Acts 2:38; 3:19) and second to be baptized in water (Matthew 28:19; Mark 16:16; John 3:22; 4:1-2; Acts 2:38, 41; 8:12, 36; 9:18; 10:48; 16:15, 33; 18:8; 19:5; 22:16; Romans 6:3; I Corinthians 1:13). To those who thus respond in genuine faith to the preaching of the gospel, God gives the gift of His Holy Spirit (Mark 1:8; Luke 24:49; John 3:5, 6; Acts 1:5; 2:1-4, 38-39; 5:32; 8:15, 17; 9:17; 10:44-47; 11:15-16; 15:8; 19:2, 6; Titus 3:5).

The phrase "Jew first" appears again in Romans. (See Romans 2:9, 10.) It does not imply ethnic superiority of Jews over non-Jews. It is simply a reference to the historical fact that the gospel of Christ was offered first to the Jewish people, then to Gentiles. (Because of the pervasive influence of Greek culture on the Roman Empire, the Jewish people considered all non-Jews as "Greeks.")

Jesus came to Israel as their Messiah, the fulfillment of all the Messianic prophecies in the Hebrew Scriptures. When the religious leaders of the Jews rejected Him, He turned to the Gentiles and began to offer Himself to them as the fulfillment of the Old Testament prophecies that the Jewish Messiah would also bring salvation to the Gentiles. Matthew 12:14-50 portrays this dramatic turn of events. It did not mean salvation was no longer available to individual Jews; it simply meant the new covenant was now available to all—regardless of ethnicity—who would believe. (See Galatians 3:28; Colossians 3:11.)

The phrase "from faith to faith" means that, from start to finish, salvation is a matter of faith. Although specific acts of obedience are involved (e.g., repentance and baptism), they are validated only by faith. A person could confess his sins and even be baptized for reasons other than faith. In that case, there is no validity either to the confession or the baptism. Jesus said, "He who believes and is baptized will be saved; but he who does not believe will be condemned" (Mark 16:16). Believing must precede any other response; indeed, all responses must be responses of faith. Jesus' statement "He who does not believe will be condemned" indicates that if a person does not believe, it does not matter what else he does; he is not saved.

Romans 1:17 is one of the three places where the New Testament quotes Habakkuk 2:4. The idea that salvation comes only through faith is central to New Testament soteriology (doctrine of salvation). This letter to the

Roman church describes the fruitlessness of the works of the law apart from faith. (See Romans 9:32.)

Each time the New Testament quotes Habakkuk 2:4, the emphasis is different. Here, the emphasis is on "faith" as opposed to the works of the law. In Galatians 3:11, the emphasis is on those who live by faith being "just" as opposed to those who live by the law (for salvation) not being justified. In Hebrews 10:38, the emphasis is on the fact that the just shall "live" by faith as opposed to the perdition that comes upon those who draw back from faith.

The Faithfulness of God

After a lengthy discussion of Israel's sinfulness in spite of the superior revelation they enjoyed (see Romans 2:1-29; 3:1-2), Romans 3:3 asks, "For what if some did not believe? Will their unbelief make the faithfulness of God without effect?" The KJV translation, "Shall their unbelief make the faith of God without effect," may lead some to think, as noted in the opening discussion of this chapter, that God has faith. But the translation offered by the NKJV accurately conveys the sense of the Greek text. The issue is not God's faith, or trust, in someone or something else; the issue is the faithfulness, or the trustworthiness, of God.

The Jewish people were the recipients of superior revelation, but some of them did not respond to it in faith. But the failure of some of the Jewish people to believe would not cause God to ignore or forget the promises He had made in the law, including the promises of judgment upon unbelievers. People may not be faithful, but God is. We can rely upon Him without reservation to do what He has said He will do.

A Covenant of Faith

After a discussion of the termination of the law of Moses as an active covenant, and the revelation of the righteousness of God apart from the law, Romans 3:22 declares, "Even the righteousness of God, which is through faith in Jesus Christ to all and on all who believe. For there is no difference."

The new covenant is a faith covenant, whereas the benefits of the old covenant came by works.[3] Under the new covenant, people enter into a right relationship with God on the basis of their faith in (trust in, reliance upon) Jesus Christ. The law of Moses focused on an elaborate system of rituals. Even under the old covenant, however, adherence to those rituals did not guarantee right standing with God; people were still saved by faith in God. (See Galatians 3:11-12; Hebrews 10:1.) The new covenant focuses on a person: Jesus Christ. Faith in Jesus Christ, complete trust in and reliance upon Him for salvation, guarantees right standing with God.

The righteousness of God revealed by the new covenant is available "to all and on all who believe." It makes no difference in terms of the new covenant if a person is a Jew or a Gentile: "there is no difference." (See Galatians 3:28.)

Faith and the Blood

God set forth Christ Jesus as "a propitiation by His blood, through faith, to demonstrate His righteousness, because in His forbearance God had passed over the sins that were previously committed, to demonstrate at the present time His righteousness, that He might be just and the justifier of the one who has faith in Jesus" (Romans 3:25-26).

The satisfaction ("propitiation") available by the blood of Jesus comes through faith. Though people were saved during the old covenant, they could not be justified by the works of the law of Moses. The phrase "because in His forbearance God had passed over the sins that were previously committed" describes the means by which God forgave the sins of those Israelites who lived between the giving of the law at Sinai and the coming of Christ. He forgave those who came to Him by faith. (See Hebrews 11:6.) He did this in anticipation of the atonement that the death of Jesus would provide.

Under the law of Moses Israel could not know Jesus Christ directly, and thus could not place their faith directly in Him. But they could have faith in God, and they could participate in the rituals that pointed to the coming Christ (Colossians 2:16-17; Hebrews 10:1). On this basis, God forgave their sins just as He today forgives the sins of those who place their faith in Jesus Christ. The Cross was God's plan for redemption from eternity (Revelation 13:8). It does not matter whether those who lived before the coming of Messiah looked ahead to the Cross in faith (Isaiah 53) or whether we look back to it, also in faith. Faith appropriates the benefits of the Cross, without regard to the age in which one happens to live.

The subject of Romans 3:25 is the righteousness of God in forgiving sins prior to the Cross, and Romans 3:26 addresses His righteousness in forgiving sins after the Cross. He justifies the person who places his faith (trust or reliance) exclusively in Jesus for salvation. To have faith in Jesus is more than giving mental assent to the historical facts about His life. Genuine trust or reliance results in specific behavioral consequences. Those who believe the gospel will obey the gospel. (See II Thessalonians 1:8.)

The Law of Faith

There is no room for boasting under the new covenant, which is the law of faith: "Where is boasting then? It is excluded. By what law? Of works? No, but by the law of faith" (Romans 3:27). Under the old covenant some found a place for boasting, for the old covenant emphasized performance. (See Luke 18:9-14.) Such boasting was not indicative of right standing with God; scrupulous adherence to the law of Moses did not produce soteriological righteousness. (See Philippians 3:4-9.) But the new covenant is a law of faith. Under it, people are counted right with God not on the basis of anything they do, but on the basis of their faith in Jesus Christ. If a person is justified by faith, he has no room to boast; he has done nothing. What he has received was given to him as a free gift.

Faith Apart from the Law

The conclusion is "that a man is justified by faith apart from the deeds of the law" (Romans 3:28). There can be no mixing of faith in Jesus Christ and the deeds of the law of Moses. To embrace the law of Moses as a means of salvation is to reject Jesus; to embrace Jesus is to recognize that the law was temporary and served its purpose in pointing Israel to the Messiah. (See Galatians 3:22-25.) Justification—right standing with God—comes by faith in Jesus rather than by reliance on the performance of the law's demands.

Faith and the One God

In a statement certain to startle Jewish readers, Romans 3:30 says, "There is one God who will justify the circumcised by faith and the uncircumcised through faith." Regardless of a person's ethnic background, justification comes only through faith in Jesus Christ. (See Romans 3:26.)

The declaration that there is one God who relates to both Jews and Gentiles through faith dramatically reveals that the radical monotheism of the Jewish people must become the radical monotheism of the Gentiles. The faith of the ancient Jews was uncompromisingly monotheistic; so was the faith of the first-century church. There was no expansion of monotheism to include some idea of plurality within God. (See Deuteronomy 6:4.)

Faith and the Law

If faith is the means of justification under the new covenant, does this "make void the law"? (Romans 3:31a). "Certainly not! On the contrary, we establish the law" (Romans 3:31b). This short statement does not negate everything this letter says elsewhere about the temporary nature of the law of Moses and its termination with the coming of the Messiah. To "establish" the law does not mean to return to the law as a requirement for life. It means to recognize the validity of the law for the purposes for which God gave it.[4] That under the new covenant we approach God by faith does not mean the old covenant was without purpose.

Abraham Believed God

Jewish readers could not deny the example of Abraham. He lived four centuries before the law was given at

Sinai, yet he was counted righteous: "For what does the Scripture say? 'Abraham believed God, and it was accounted to him for righteousness'" (Romans 4:3). (See also Romans 4:9.) God imputed righteousness to Abraham based on his faith. This verse quotes Genesis 15:6 and, at that point in Abraham's life, he had not yet received the promised son. He had believed God's Word and by faith He had obeyed God's command to leave his homeland and come to the land of promise, but he had done nothing that could earn his salvation.

Some may think that Romans at this point disputes James's teaching that Abraham was justified by works (James 2:21-23). But the problem is merely one of perception. In Romans "faith" is a genuine trust in God that results in obedience to God's commands; the "faith" of the Book of James is at best mental assent with no evidence of genuineness. In Romans, "works" are activities done to gain favor with God; in James "works" are the natural consequences of genuinely held belief. There is no thought in James that the works resulting from faith somehow enhance one's standing with God. They are simply the logical actions and the inevitable fruit of one who is already in good standing with God.

In addition, Romans and James have reference to two different episodes in the life of Abraham. Romans describes Abraham's response of complete, trusting belief in God's words when He said, "Look now toward heaven, and count the stars if you are able to number them. . . . So shall your descendants be" (Genesis 15:5). Abraham "believed in the Lord, and He accounted it to him for righteousness" (Genesis 15:6). God knows, even before a person has had the opportunity to demonstrate his faith, whether it is genuine.

But James deals with another matter. It describes the manner in which Abraham demonstrated genuine faith throughout his life in contrast to those who claim it is possible to possess faith without ever giving evidence of it. Though God did not wait to justify Abraham until he had obediently offered his son, Abraham's obedience to the Lord's command demonstrated the genuineness of the faith he already possessed.

The Book of James does not imply that Abraham was not justified in the sight of God until he offered Isaac on the altar; it points out that Abraham's obedience to God's command demonstrated the validity of his faith and illustrated before others the right standing he already possessed with God.

It is important to note that Abraham did not offer his son in an attempt to earn favor with God. If that had been his motive, both Romans and James would reveal his actions to be inadequate. But for a person who genuinely trusts God, there is no reasonable alternative to obedience to God. Since one has already placed his faith in God, he does not debate on a day-by-day basis whether he should obey any specific command of God. If one's trust is in God, there is no other course of action but to obey Him.

Faith and Righteousness

Romans 4:4-5 displays the contrast between relying on works and faith: "Now to him who works, the wages are not counted as grace but as debt. But to him who does not work but believes on Him who justifies the ungodly, his faith is accounted for righteousness."

Under the law of Moses, the rewards received were

not free (grace) gifts, but wages (debt) due for services rendered. Only if salvation is free can it be a gift. Otherwise, it is something God owes us. If the latter were true, our salvation would glorify us, not God.

But people can receive right standing with God only as a gift by faith. This does not mean that a person with faith will do nothing; it means that he does not rely on his works to earn right standing with God.

The faith required for salvation is not some general kind of belief; it must be belief "on Him who justifies the ungodly." God observes the faith of the ungodly person and responds by imputing the righteousness of Jesus Christ to his account.

A Seal of the Righteousness of Faith

Abraham's righteousness was not connected to any work performed: "And he received the sign of circumcision, a seal of the righteousness of the faith which he had while still uncircumcised, that he might be the father of all those who believe, though they are uncircumcised, that righteousness might be imputed to them also" (Romans 4:11).

As important as it was to Abraham and his descendants, circumcision was merely a seal of the faith, and the right standing with God consequent to faith, that Abraham already possessed. And since circumcision was an outward, physical work, it was possible that a Jewish man could be circumcised completely apart from faith. (See Romans 2:26-29.) Just because a man was circumcised, that was no sign he was a man of faith. But, under the law, if he was a man of faith, he would be circumcised.

The reason God counted Abraham righteous on the

basis of his faith before his circumcision was so that Abraham could be the father of *all* those who believe, including uncircumcised Gentiles. Indeed, Jewish men themselves, in order to be counted right with God, had to do more than to be circumcised; they had to "walk in the steps of the faith" their father Abraham had prior to his circumcision (Romans 4:12). Since Jewish boys were circumcised on the eighth day, their circumcision alone said nothing about their faith in God.

A Promise through Faith

The law of Moses had nothing to do with the Abrahamic covenant. (See Galatians 3:15-18.) "For the promise that he would be the heir of the world was not to Abraham or to his seed through the law, but through the righteousness of faith" (Romans 4:13). Any attempt to merge faith and law is doomed: "For if those who are of the law are heirs, faith is made void and the promise made of no effect" (Romans 4:14). Since Gentiles were never under the law of Moses, it was necessary that the Abrahamic covenant—which included blessings upon Gentiles—be completely independent of the law: "Therefore it is of faith that it might be according to grace, so that the promise might be sure to all the seed, not only to those who are of the law, but also to those who are of the faith of Abraham, who is the father of us all" (Romans 4:16). The phrase "all the seed" includes believing Gentiles as well as Jews.

Abraham Believed God

God promised Abraham that he would be the father of many nations: "(As it is written, 'I have made you a father of many nations') in the presence of Him whom he believed, even God, who gives life to the dead and calls those things which do not exist as though they did" (Romans 4:17). (See Genesis 17:5). This promise is fulfilled in that Abraham is father not only to his believing physical descendants, but also to believing Gentiles.

Abraham had to believe in a God who gives life to the dead and calls things that do not exist as though they did because Abraham was physically unable to beget a child (Romans 4:19). When he received God's promise, he had no children at all. Yet God gave life (the ability to reproduce) to Abraham and Sarah. Since God knew the future, He called Abraham the father of many nations before Abraham had any children. This is what Scripture means by God calling "those things which do not exist as though they did." There is no hint here of the "word of faith" teaching, which suggests that we human beings can "speak things into existence." As this verse clearly says, only God can give life to the dead and call those things that do not exist as though they did. He knows the end from the beginning.

We should note that the idea of Abraham being the father of many nations originated with God, not Abraham. Faith is our response to God's initiative, not vice versa.

Hoping Against Hope

Abraham demonstrated faith in that, though he had no earthly reason to hope for a son much less to be the father of many nations, he hoped anyway, because he had God's promise: "Who, contrary to hope, in hope believed, so that he became the father of many nations, according to what was spoken, 'So shall your descendants be'"

(Romans 4:18). It is essential to realize that his hope was not mere wishful thinking. He was responding to the promise of God. There is no basis here for so-called "positive thinking" or "possibility thinking." These psychological techniques may have their place, but God does not chart His course based on our positive mental attitude. If God had not promised Abraham that he would be the father of many nations, Abraham could have visualized, set goals, and talked as if he had many children as long as he wished, but it would have been fruitless. But when God speaks, no matter how impossible a situation may seem, there is reason for hope. God's promise overwhelms impossibilities.

Strengthened in Faith

Abraham was strong in his faith. This strength was demonstrated in that he did not even consider his or Sarah's physical inability to reproduce: "And not being weak in faith, he did not consider his own body, already dead (since he was about a hundred years old), and the deadness of Sarah's womb. He did not waver at the promise of God through unbelief, but was strengthened in faith, giving glory to God, and being fully convinced that what He had promised He was also able to perform" (Romans 4:19-21). Abraham knew that if God had spoken, He would keep His promise. He never wavered in his faith. Instead, his faith increased as he gave glory to God in advance for what God had promised to do.

It may seem strange that Romans would make these claims about Abraham, in that Abraham did go into Hagar, by whom he fathered Ishmael. But this was Sarah's idea, and as strange as it seems to us, it was quite according to the customs of the time. (See Genesis 16.) According to Romans, Abraham did not waver in his belief that God would give him the promised seed, even though he wrongly followed Sarah's advice to father a child by Hagar. Abraham was fully convinced that God was able to do what He had promised.

Why This Story Was Written
Scripture does not record the account of Abraham for the sake of Abraham alone; it does so for the sake of new covenant believers: "Now it was not written for his sake alone that it was imputed to him, but also for us. It shall be imputed to us who believe in Him who raised up Jesus our Lord from the dead" (Romans 4:23-24). Abraham's example should help Jewish and Gentile Christians understand that God will impute righteousness to them on the same basis as He did to Abraham: by faith. The only difference is the *content* of their faith. Abraham believed God's promise concerning a promised son; in the new covenant we believe in the God who raised Jesus up from the dead. This is, of course, the same God in whom Abraham believed, but he was not privileged to receive the revelation of the resurrected Messiah.

The Result of Justification by Faith
The right standing with God we enjoy by our faith in Jesus Christ results in peace with God: "Therefore, having been justified by faith, we have peace with God through our Lord Jesus Christ" (Romans 5:1). The separation from fellowship with God that results from our sins is replaced by His acceptance of us. The enmity between God and humanity is removed. Because of the death of

Jesus, there is no reason for any person to remain separated from God. As far as God is concerned, every barrier has been removed, because the blood of Jesus dealt conclusively with the sin problem.

In that sense, sin is no longer a problem. The question now is not, *What will you do about your sins*, but *What will you do with Jesus?* From God's perspective, the world is reconciled to Him: "That is, that God was in Christ reconciling the world to Himself, not imputing their trespasses to them, and has committed to us the word of reconciliation. Therefore we are ambassadors for Christ, as though God were pleading through us: we implore you on Christ's behalf, be reconciled to God" (II Corinthians 5:19-20). Through Christ, God has been reconciled to the world. All that remains is for the world to be reconciled to Him.

The only people who will suffer eternal condemnation are those who do not avail themselves of the provisions made in the blood of Jesus. By their rejection of Him, they will cause their sins to be imputed, or counted, to their record. But those who by faith receive the benefits of the Atonement are justified. Their sins are not imputed to them. Since there are no sins on their record, they enjoy peace with God.

Access of Faith

Faith is fundamental to gain access to God: "Through whom also we have access by faith into this grace in which we stand, and rejoice in hope of the glory of God" (Romans 5:2). (See Hebrews 11:6.) Our trust in Jesus gains us entrance into the grace of God, where we receive such assurance of our salvation that we rejoice in hope.

Biblical hope is not wishful thinking; it is the absolute assurance that what God has promised He will perform.

We Believe We Will Live with Him

Romans 6:8 restates a truth first addressed in Romans 6:4-5: "Now if we died with Christ, we believe that we shall also live with Him." Identification with Jesus Christ in His death results in identification with Him in His life: "Therefore we were buried with him through baptism into death, that just as Christ was raised from the dead by the glory of the Father, even so we also should walk in newness of life. For if we have been united together in the likeness of His death, certainly we also shall be in the likeness of His resurrection" (Romans 6:4-5). Galatians 2:20 makes exactly the same point: "I have been crucified with Christ; it is no longer I who live, but Christ lives in me; and the life which I now live in the flesh I live by faith in the Son of God, who loved me and gave Himself for me."

In Romans 6:8, the word "believe" describes the conviction or trust believers have that they will indeed live with Christ, just as surely as they have died and been buried with Him. There may be an ultimate reference here to the bodily resurrection of the believer and to eternal life in the presence of God, but the immediate and contextual concern is apparently for the believer's life on earth, or, as Galatians 2:20 says, "in the flesh." In other words, just as believers are united with Christ in His death and burial here and now, so are they united with Him in His life.

Pursue Right Standing with God by Faith

Many statements in Romans no doubt shocked first-century Jewish believers. One of them is Romans 9:30-

32: "What shall we say then? That Gentiles, who did not pursue righteousness, have attained to righteousness, even the righteousness of faith; but Israel, pursuing the law of righteousness, has not attained to the law of righteousness. Why? Because they did not seek it by faith, but as it were, by the works of the law. For they stumbled at that stumbling stone."

This passage is key to understanding the contrast between the law of Moses (the old covenant, Hebrews 8:13) and the new covenant. An error here sends the student of Scripture down the wrong path in grasping the biblical teaching on the purpose for which the law was given and its radical distinction from the covenant established in the blood of Jesus (Matthew 26:28).

The Gentiles mentioned in this passage were Gentile Christians who, prior to the coming of Jesus, made no attempt to pursue righteousness. But when they heard the gospel, they believed in Jesus and thus attained right standing (righteousness) with God by faith.

The Israel in view is national Israel, not individual Jews who did believe on Jesus. In general, the Jews pursued the law of righteousness, but they did not attain it. It is important to note here that the word "law" is modified by the word "righteousness," which is in the genitive case and serves to describe the law. In other words, the point is not simply that Israel pursued the law of Moses but did not attain it. Paul himself declared that, prior to his coming to Christ, he was blameless concerning the righteousness that is in the law (Philippians 3:6), which he identified as self-righteousness (Philippians 3:9). Zacharias and Elizabeth, the parents of John the Baptist, walked "in all the commandments and ordinances of the

Lord blameless" (Luke 1:6). Romans 9:31 does not suggest that Israel was unsuccessful in keeping the law of Moses; it declares they were unsuccessful in attaining the law *of righteousness*.

The reason for Israel's failure was that they did not seek it (the context defines the object of their search as the law of righteousness) by faith, but by the works of the law, a term that refers to the entirety of the law of Moses. The stumbling stone at which they stumbled was the Messiah, Jesus. Rather than placing their faith in Him, they continued to seek right standing with God by the law of Moses, even though God never intended the law of Moses to provide right standing with God.[5]

Elsewhere, Paul declared under divine inspiration, "I do not set aside the grace of God; for if righteousness comes through the law, then Christ died in vain" (Galatians 2:21). He also wrote, "You have become estranged from Christ, you who attempt to be justified by law; you have fallen from grace" (Galatians 5:4). Romans 9:30-32 cannot mean, then, that soteriological righteousness was available by the works of the law of Moses but that Israel simply failed to keep the law perfectly. The point is that they pursued the law *of righteousness*, or righteousness itself, by the works of the law of Moses, and the two are mutually incompatible.

It may at first seem strange to distinguish between the law of righteousness and the law of Moses, but words are defined by their context and the manner in which they are used. "Law" (Greek, *nomos*) has a wide range of meaning in both testaments. In this case, the use of "law" in Romans 9:31 is influenced both by the previous verse, where righteousness is the object of pursuit by believing

Gentiles, and by the genitive modifier "of righteousness" in the immediate phrase. The word "law" is sometimes a very general reference to Scripture at large.[6] The point here is that, unlike the Gentiles prior to the coming of Messiah, Israel did pursue right standing with God, but they did not attain it because they sought it by the works of the law of Moses rather than by faith.

Some have offered a different interpretation of this passage, indicating that the law of Moses has continuing application to the church, but the first-century church did not seem to retain the law of Moses in any degree.[7] Another suggestion is that when Romans speaks of the "works of the law" here it refers not to the demands of the law itself but to the law as misinterpreted by Pharisaic Judaism, or legalism. To sustain this idea, C. E. B. Cranfield has suggested that the first-century Greek language used by Paul had no term for legalism and that Paul was thus unable to clarify his meaning.[8] But, as D. A. Carson points out, Cranfield has committed the word-study fallacy of appealing to an unknown or unlikely meaning. Although it is argued that "law" sometimes means legalism, "the fact remains that the primary defense of that position is not rigorous linguistic evidence but the adoption of a certain structure of relationships between the Old Testament and the New."[9] Stephen Westerholm also rejects this idea, calling the argument "specious" and pointing out that "whether or not the Greek language possessed a suitable single word for 'legalism,' it surely provided, and Paul's vocabulary included, sufficient resources for indicating whether he was speaking of the law as intended by God or in the (allegedly) perverted form in which it was regarded by Jews."[10]

To interpret Romans 9:31-32 in harmony with the rest of Scripture on the same subject, the meaning must be that Israel failed to attain righteousness because she sought it by the works of the law rather than by faith. Otherwise it would be virtually impossible to make sense of statements like Galatians 3:11-12: "But that no one is justified by the law in the sight of God is evident, for 'The just shall live by faith.' Yet the law is not of faith, but 'the man who does them shall live by them.'" There is no clue here that Galatians means no one is justified by legalism because legalism is not of faith. If that is the meaning, it would appear to be wrong to quote Leviticus 18:5 as support. Furthermore, Christ did not die to redeem us from the curse of legalism, but from the curse of the law (Galatians 3:10, 13).

As Gary Tuck has pointed out, "Israel's failure was her looking in the wrong place for righteousness. *Her appeal to the law (and its works) for righteousness was itself an act of unbelief* (which blinded her to Messiah when he came)."[11] The problem is not that Israel should have but did not respond to the law by faith; the law was a works covenant to which a works response was entirely appropriate. The problem is that Israel should have responded to *God* by faith. If Israel had been responding to God by faith at the time of the coming of the Messiah, the nation would have believed on Jesus.[12]

There were many people of faith in ancient Israel prior to the coming of the Messiah. (See Hebrews 11:27-38.) These people were justified *by faith* (Hebrews 11:39), not by the works of the law. Those who did have faith in God demonstrated the genuineness of their faith by their adherence to the terms of the law of Moses. But nowhere does either testament suggest that any person of faith gained right standing with God by the works of the law; their righteousness came by their faith.[13]

A Stone in Zion

Israel's failure to attain right standing with God was due to their lack of faith in God and their reliance upon the works of the law. Their faithlessness and focus on works caused them to stumble. The stumbling stone was none other than Jesus Christ Himself: "As it is written: 'Behold, I lay in Zion a stumbling stone and rock of offense, and whoever believes on Him will not be put to shame'" (Romans 9:33). This verse quotes from both Isaiah 8:14 and 28:16 (Septuagint) to summarize the point of the entire chapter: (1) Those who are offended by the idea of free salvation brought by means of the Messiah's atonement will fall and be broken. (See Isaiah 8:15.) (2) Those who believe on Him will not be disappointed; their faith will be rewarded.

The End of the Law for Believers

Paul was keenly interested in the salvation of national Israel (Romans 10:1). The Jewish people had a zeal for God, but their zeal was not based on accurate knowledge about how to attain right standing with God (Romans 10:2-3). They sought to establish their own righteousness by relying upon the works of the law (Romans 9:32; 10:3). They did not realize that right standing with God is given to every person who believes on Jesus Christ: "For Christ is the end of the law for righteousness to everyone who believes" (Romans 10:4).[14] Trusting in one's own ability to adhere to the works of the law is essentially self-confidence (Philippians 3:9); to trust in Jesus Christ for one's right standing with God is faith.

The Righteousness of Faith

The righteousness that sprang from adherence to the law of Moses was not soteriological: "For Moses writes about the righteousness which is of the law, 'The man who does those things shall live by them'" (Romans 10:5).[15] The old covenant emphasized *doing*. The life promised to those who were obedient to the law of Moses was not eternal life, but a certain quality of life in the land promised to Abraham.

Romans contrasts the righteousness of the law with the righteousness of faith: "But the righteousness of faith speaks in this way, 'Do not say in your heart, "Who will ascend into heaven?"' (that is, to bring Christ down from above) or, '"Who will descend into the abyss?"' (that is, to bring Christ up from the dead)" (Romans 10:6-7).[16] The right standing with God that comes by faith does not focus on what a person can do, but on what Jesus Christ has already done on behalf of humanity. Under inspiration of the Holy Spirit, Paul adapted the Septuagint translation of Deuteronomy 30:12-14 to apply to the Incarnation (bringing Christ down from above) and the Resurrection (bringing Christ up from the dead). Faith makes no attempt to force the hand of God; faith simply trusts what He has already done. Faith does not assume responsibility for the Incarnation or Resurrection, or, for that matter, for doing any other good work in an attempt to gain favor with God. Faith focuses on what God has done.

Romans 10:5 is not the only place where Scripture quotes Leviticus 18:5 to demonstrate that the law of

Moses was not a covenant of faith, but of works.[17] Galatians 3:12 says, "Yet the law is not of faith, but 'the man who does them shall live by them.'" Thus, "the righteousness which is of the law" (Romans 10:5) is not faith righteousness. It is a works righteousness wherein a person gained right standing with his fellow man by his deeds (e.g., Deuteronomy 24:13), and the New Testament contrasts it with the right standing with God that springs from faith.

Some have suggested that there is no contrast between the "righteousness which is of the law" and the "righteousness of faith" in Romans 10:5-6. According to this view, Romans 10 refers to soteriological righteousness being available under the law to those who kept the law of Moses by faith. Thus, Leviticus 18:5 is taken to mean that the "man does, [by faith] shall live [eternally] by them." It is pointed out that the adversative "but" in Romans 10:6 is translated from the weaker *de* rather than the stronger *alla*, implying that in some way both verses are describing the same kind of righteousness.

It seems that the greatest reason for this interpretation is the problem perceived in contrasting two mutually exclusive ways of attaining righteousness: on the basis of law or on the basis of faith. But the following objections render this view unlikely:

If there is no contrast between the "righteousness which is of the law" and the "righteousness of faith," Paul in Galatians is pitted against Paul in Romans. Galatians 3:11-12 says, "But that no one is justified by the law in the sight of God is evident, for 'the just shall live by faith.' Yet the law is not of faith, but 'the man who does them shall live by them.'" This passage quotes the same verse as Romans 10:5 does, namely Leviticus 18:5. It does so to demonstrate that "the law is not of faith," that is, the law of Moses is not a faith covenant. To resolve this problem, those who see no contrast in Romans 10:5-6 suggest that Galatians uses the word "law" to refer, not to the law of Moses, but to a Jewish misinterpretation of the law, or legalism. As noted earlier, this is a word-study fallacy appealing to an unknown or unlikely meaning, and contextually this idea will not work.[18]

The suggestion that there is no contrast between "the righteousness which is of the law" and "the righteousness of faith" fails to notice that the righteousness of the law was not soteriological, whereas the righteousness of faith is soteriological. It is true that the words "righteousness" and "life" appear in the section of the Pentateuch dealing with the law of Moses. But it is also true that words are defined by their contexts, and there is no indication in the covenant established at Sinai that the righteousness in view had anything to do with salvation. Nor is there any evidence that the life in view was eternal life. The righteousness attained on the basis of the works of the law was horizontally relational, not vertically. That is, it had to do with one's relationship with his fellow man; adherence to the works of the law did not result in right standing with God. The life promised in the law was not eternal life, but long life in the land promised to the patriarchs. A contextual view of these key terms in Deuteronomy supports this premise.[19]

The objection that Romans 10:6 uses the adversative *de* rather than the stronger *alla* suggests that Romans 10:6 is merely a continuation of Romans 10:5. In other words, the righteousness of faith is identical to the righteousness of the law. It seems certain, however, in view of the immediate context, the use of Leviticus 18:5 in Galatians 3:12, and the larger scope of the teaching on this subject, that this is not the case. Although *de* may, in some cases, mean "and," *de* can just as legitimately mean "on the other hand" or "but." Its translation as "but" in the leading and most reputable translations is surely justified.

The Preached Word of Faith

Instead of attempting to participate in its own salvation by claiming human merit for the incarnation or resurrection of the Messiah (see Romans 10:6-7), the righteousness of faith declares, "The word is near you, even in your mouth and in your heart" (Romans 10:8a). What is so near as to be in one's mouth and heart is "the word of faith which we preach" (Romans 10:8b). The word of faith has nothing to do with positive confession, as it is sometimes defined. It refers rather to the good news of justification by faith. Paul declared the word of faith was something "we preach." The word he declared, especially in the letter to the Romans, was justification by faith.

Believing in Your Heart

We see the connection between genuine faith and confession in Romans 10:9-10: "That if you confess with your mouth the Lord Jesus and believe in your heart that God has raised Him from the dead, you will be saved. For with the heart one believes to righteousness, and with the mouth confession is made to salvation." Verse 9 first mentions the confession of the mouth, then the belief in one's heart; verse 10 reverses the order. Verse 9 merely presents the facts that lead to salvation: they include confession of the mouth and belief in the heart in the resurrection of Christ. Verse 10 presents the order in which these occur: faith must precede the confession. Thus, faith is the *cause* of the confession. The confession springs from faith, just as faith is the impetus for all valid works.[20]

No Shame for Those Who Believe
Quoting again from Isaiah 28:16 (see Romans 9:33), Romans 10:11-13 says, "For the Scripture says, 'Whoever believes on Him will not be put to shame.' For there is no distinction between Jew and Greek, for the same Lord over all is rich to all who call upon Him. For 'whoever calls upon the name of the LORD shall be saved.'" Faith in Jesus Christ will never fail to produce the desired result.

"Whoever" includes Gentiles as well as Jews. The new covenant does not extend benefits exclusively to Jews. (See Romans 2:26-29.) Rather, it dissolves the distinction between Jew and Greek (i.e., Gentile). (See also Galatians 3:28; Colossians 3:11; Ephesians 2:15-18.)

Salvation is available to all on the basis of faith as expressed by calling on the name of the Lord. (See Joel 2:32; Acts 2:21.) To call on the name of the Lord is to call on the Lord Himself. Inherent in calling on the name of the Lord is calling on Him for deliverance and salvation.

Hearing, Believing, Calling
Salvation requires a specific order of events: "How then shall they call on Him in whom they have not believed? And how shall they believe in Him of whom they have not heard? And how shall they hear without a preacher?" (Romans 10:14). Here again we see the order

of Romans 10:10: first one believes, then he calls.

This order disproves the psychological theories that suggest "feeling follows action." If this idea were true, there would be value in calling on the name of the Lord prior to and apart from faith. But it is faith that validates all else. It may be true that certain actions are so closely identified with emotional currents that some very shallow feelings result from a person's acting as if he felt a certain way, but doing so is far different from actions that spring from genuine, deep-seated commitments and love.

A person cannot call on the Lord and receive any salvific benefit if the call is not based on faith. And a person cannot have faith in the Lord if he has never heard of Him. And it is impossible to hear of Him apart from a "preacher." The word "preacher" is translated from a form of the Greek *kerusso*, which means "to proclaim." A person cannot hear if there is no proclamation.

Faith Comes by Hearing

Some have heard but have not obeyed: "But they have not all obeyed the gospel. For Isaiah says, 'Lord, who has believed our report?' So then faith comes by hearing, and hearing by the word of God'" (Romans 10:16-17). This passage includes a quote from the central atonement section of the Hebrew Scriptures, Isaiah 53:1. The nation of Israel should have anticipated the suffering Messiah of Isaiah 53, and they should have welcomed Him, because their own Scriptures announced the good news of His coming and of His substitutionary sacrifice.

A textual variant in verse 17 reads "hearing by the word of [about] Christ." Contextually, this idea seems correct. Faith comes as a result of hearing the good news ("word" is translated from a form of the Greek *rhema,* which means "a saying") of the coming Messiah. It is, of course, possible to hear this good news and reject it, as Romans 10:18-21 indicates. Although faith may come or be increased by reading the Scriptures or by hearing biblical preaching or teaching, this verse refers to the specific word of the gospel message.

Standing by Faith

Those Jewish people who were "broken off" the olive tree, which represents Abrahamic blessing, lost their status because of unbelief; those Gentiles who were "grafted in" received this privilege by faith: "You will say then, 'Branches were broken off that I might be grafted in.' Well said. Because of unbelief they were broken off, and you stand by faith. Do not be haughty, but fear. For if God did not spare the natural branches, He may not spare you either" (Romans 11:19-21).

Some Gentile believers might be tempted to boast by saying, "Branches [Israelites] were broken off that I might be grafted in." Such a claim of spiritual superiority or elitism is reprehensible. (See Galatians 3:28; Colossians 3:11; Ephesians 2:11-22.) The reason some of the branches were broken off was because of their unbelief in Jesus the Messiah, and the only reason Gentiles were grafted in was because of their faith in Jesus the Messiah. This fact should not inspire pride on the Gentiles' part, but fear of God, for if God broke off the "natural branches" (physical descendants of Abraham) because of their unbelief, He will not hesitate to break off those who are not natural branches if they fail to believe.

Thinking Soberly

It is a human tendency to think highly of ourselves. But we should not base our view of ourselves on our own assessment, but on the faith given by God: "For I say, through the grace given to me, to everyone who is among you, not to think of himself more highly than he ought to think, but to think soberly, as God has dealt to each one a measure of faith" (Romans 12:3). Each believer must carefully evaluate his own giftedness and place of ministry in the body of Christ by means of the faith given by God. This evaluation has nothing to do with visualization, positive thinking, or even with goal setting. This passage calls for sober reflection and assessment of the gifts and abilities one possesses by the grace of God. Since faith is essentially trust, one can evaluate his giftedness by determining for which of the seven areas of service (verse 6-7) he is able to trust God.[21]

Weak in Faith

Romans 14:1 introduces the idea that a person can be a believer but be weak in the faith: "Receive one who is weak in the faith, but not to disputes over doubtful things." The issue is not the believer's salvation, but his inability to participate in biblically acceptable behavior because of a "weak" conscience.

I Corinthians 8 discusses a similar issue. The Corinthian church had written to Paul asking a series of questions (I Corinthians 7:1). One of them was whether it was right to eat meat that had been offered to idols (I Corinthians 8:4). Paul's response four times identified those who were condemned by the eating of such meat as having a "weak conscience" (I Corinthians 8:7, 9-10, 12). The issue here in Romans 14 is practically identical.

The admonition to the Roman church was that they were to receive one another as brethren of equal value, equally acceptable to the Lord in spite of their differences. Their acceptance of one another was not to be a mere facade for "disputes over doubtful things."

God did not expect the church at Rome to have unanimity on the subjects discussed in this chapter. It is clear from the discussion that there is room in the church for differences of opinion on nonessential issues. For this room to exist, however, all believers must be willing to recognize that not everything is essential, no matter how strongly some opinions are held.

A specific disagreement between believers in Rome was that some in good conscience placed no restriction on their diet, while others—the weak—were vegetarians: "For one believes he may eat all things, but he who is weak eats only vegetables" (Romans 14:2). The text does not explain why these believers were vegetarians. Other passages of Scripture discuss the eating of meat offered to idols (Acts 15:29; I Corinthians 8; 10:16-30; Revelation 2:14, 20). It could be that these vegetarians had adopted that practice so as to avoid any possibility of eating meat that had been offered to idols.

Whatever their reason, their position was unnecessary; they were "weak in the faith." (See Genesis 9:3; Mark 7:19; I Timothy 4:1-5.) The conscience of these weak believers was the victim of incorrect information. The instincts of their conscience did not fit biblical reality. Nevertheless, they held their conviction sincerely, and it is certainly not wrong to abstain from meat.

The person whose faith is stronger and who is thus able to participate in biblically approved behavior is a happy person: "Do you have faith? Have it to yourself before God. Happy is he who does not condemn himself in what he approves" (Romans 14:22). But if the stronger brother has faith (trust in God) to engage in practices that weaker brothers condemn but Scripture does not, he is to keep his liberty between him and God. If he is not condemned by his liberties, he is a happy person. Herein we see God's overriding concern: He wants believers to live free from condemnation, because condemnation distracts a person from full and free fellowship with God, even if it is caused by an ill-informed conscience.

But if a weaker brother does not believe it is right to participate in a certain activity, even though Scripture does not condemn the activity specifically or in principle, he will be condemned if he participates in the activity: "But he who doubts is condemned if he eats, because he does not eat from faith; for whatever is not from faith is sin" (Romans 14:23). The KJV translation is "damned," but the word here does not refer to loss of salvation, so the better translation is "condemned." The reason for this condemnation is that the weaker brother is not participating in the activity out of faith, or trust in God. He cannot trust God that the activity is acceptable to Him. The condemnation he experiences is not from God; it is self-condemnation.

"For whatever is not from faith is sin" does not mean that participation in biblically acceptable behavior is a sin in the eyes of God. If that were true, we would never be certain what sin is, and Scripture would no longer be our final authority. The word "sin" (*hamartia*) simply means "to miss the mark." It may mean God's mark of perfection, but it may also mean a mark we have established for ourselves.

For example, among the ancient people of Gibeah were seven hundred left-handed men who could sling a stone at a hair's breadth and not miss (Judges 20:15-16). The Hebrew word translated "not miss" is the same as the word commonly translated "sin." Like *hamartia*, it means "to miss the mark." In the case of the weaker brother, he has set a mark of behavior for himself that he believes is necessary; if he falls short of that mark, he condemns himself and counts himself to have sinned. This so clouds his relationship with God that it would be better for him to embrace unnecessary limitations on his behavior and live free from condemnation and a consciousness of sin than to violate his conscience to engage in the liberties of the stronger brother.

Joy and Peace in Believing

Toward the close of the letter, we find this statement: "Now may the God of hope fill you with all joy and peace in believing, that you may abound in hope by the power of the Holy Spirit" (Romans 15:13). Twice this verse mentions hope. (See also Romans 15:4.) No doubt it provides another link in the ongoing attempt to restore to the Roman believers the hope damaged by their faulty theology and perhaps by the sufferings they endured for the cause of Christ.[22]

Whereas Romans 15:5 identifies God as "the God of patience and comfort," verse 13 now identifies Him as "the God of hope." Obviously, these qualities were missing or at least diminished among the Roman believers. Paul's prayer was that as the believers' hope was restored, it would result in joy and peace in "believing" (faith). Since the Roman Christians were rich in faith (see Romans 1:8), there was no reason for them to be lacking in hope.

Faith, hope, and love are meant to accompany each other. (See I Corinthians 13:13.) The point is clear: Where there is no hope, there can be no joy or peace. There is little reason to focus on an attempt to restore joy or peace when they are missing. The restoration of hope will be accompanied by a deep inner joy and peace based on the assurance that God is in control and that He is doing all things after the counsel of His own will. (See Ephesians 1:11.)

Paul wished for his reader's hope to abound by the power of the Holy Spirit. This is an appropriate conclusion to the section of the letter dealing with practical Christianity. We can do nothing apart from the power of the indwelling Holy Spirit. (See Romans 15:19.) We cannot create our own hope; it will not result from a mere change in thinking. It will come as we rely upon the power of the Holy Spirit within.

The Obedience of Faith

Romans 16:26 proclaims, "But now has been made manifest, and by the prophetic Scriptures has been made known to all nations, according to the commandment of the everlasting God, for obedience to the faith." The NKJV translates *hypakoen pisteos* as "obedience to the faith." This takes *pisteos* as an objective genitive, and the faith in view is thus the teaching or doctrine concerning the gospel of Christ.

But the KJV translates the phrase "the obedience of faith," in which case the faith describes the kind of obedience in view. It is obedience that springs from faith. Only faith validates everything a person does in response to the preaching of the gospel.

Notes

[1]H. E. Dana and Julius R. Mantey, *A Manual Grammar of the Greek New Testament* (New York: Macmillan Publishing Co., 1955), 78-79.

[2]Wesley J. Perschbacher, *Refresh Your Greek* (Chicago: Moody Press, 1989), 1075.

[3]See page 59, note 15.

[4]See discussion under "The Law Established" in chapter 2.

[5]See discussion under "Hearing and Doing" in chapter 1.

[6]See discussion under "A Broader View of 'Law'" in chapter 2.

[7]See, e.g., Acts 15:1, 5, 10, 19, 24, 28; Galatians 1:6-9; 2:3-5, 11-16, 19, 21; 3:1-5, 10-25; 4:5, 9-11, 19-31; 5:1-6; Hebrews 3:1-6; 7:11-19, 22; 8:6-13; 9:9-22; 10:1-4, 9; 12:18-24.

[8]C. E. B. Cranfield, "St. Paul and the Law," *Scottish Journal of Theology* 17 (1964): 55.

[9]D. A. Carson, *Exegetical Fallacies* (Grand Rapids, MI: Baker Book House, 1984), 37-38.

[10]Stephen Westerholm, *Israel's Law and the Church's Faith: Paul and His Recent Interpreters* (Grand Rapids, MI: Eerdmans, 1988), 132-34.

[11]Gary Earl Tuck, "The Purpose of the Law Relative to Sin in Pauline Literature," Th.D. dissertation, Dallas Theological Seminary, 1991, 122-23.

[12]See Tuck, 123.

[13]In Romans 9:31-32, the critical text omits the words "of righteousness" in their final appearance from verse 31 and "of the law" in verse 32. The critical text follows, as is typical, the shorter reading found in some Greek manuscripts. The comments in this work follow the Majority Text. Following the reading of the critical text raises seemingly unresolvable difficulties. The text would say Israel pursued the "law of righteousness" but failed to attain to "the law" because they sought it by "works" and not by faith. This would suggest that the law of Moses is somehow a law of righteousness, in spite of all the New Testament says to the contrary, and that Israel failed to attain to the law itself because of their reliance upon works rather than faith. But the law of Moses specifically demanded works, indeed, perfect obedience. If keeping the law of Moses

by faith would have produced righteousness, we are at a loss to explain passages of Scripture like Galatians 2:21; 3:11-12, 21; Romans 3:20-22. To disregard the significance of these references by claiming they refer not to the law of Moses but to the law as misinterpreted by Judaism (legalism) is to force a meaning on Scripture that is not apparent in Scripture itself and that makes problematic all the scriptural declarations of the termination of the law with the coming of Christ.

[14]See discussion under "Christ: The End of the Law" in chapter 1.

[15]See discussion under "The Law's Righteousness Is Based on Performance" in chapter 2 and under "The Righteousness of the Law" in chapter 1.

[16]See discussion under "The Righteousness of Faith" in chapter 1.

[17]See page 59, note 15.

[18]See discussion under "Pursue Right Standing with God by Faith" earlier in this chapter.

[19]See discussion under "The Righteousness of the Law" in chapter 1.

[20]See discussion of this passage under "The Righteousness of Faith" in chapter 1.

[21]See discussion of the motivational gifts under "Seven Gifts of Grace" in chapter 3.

[22]See discussion under "Faith's Companions: Hope and Love" earlier in this chapter.

Holiness: Separating unto God And from Sin

Although the Book of Romans does not develop this theme as fully as others, it does place an emphasis on the concept of holiness. In one passage that mentions the word only twice (Romans 6), holiness is nevertheless the theme.

The Greek *hagios* is translated "holy" six times and "saints" eight times. The related *hagiazo* is once translated "sanctified." *Hagios* is the virtual equivalent of the Hebrew *qadosh*, which the Old Testament uses many times. The essential idea of *qadosh* is separation of some kind. Like any other word, it is defined by its context. *Qadosh* does not inherently imply virtue or morality.[1] When used of God, *qadosh* has to do with His separateness from the created realm. This includes, of course, separation from sin. When it is used of people in the context of relationship to the true God, it has to do first with separation *unto* Him and then, by implication, of separation *from* all that is unlike Him.

In the New Testament, we should understand the word "holy" in this sense. It has to do with separation unto God. Of necessity, this requires separation from sin. The word "saints" describes those who are separated. "Sanctification" describes the process of separation itself, whether the positional sanctification that occurs instantly at the new birth (e.g., I Corinthians 1:2; 6:11) or the progressive growth in sanctification that occurs as the believer daily seeks to come into greater conformity to the character of Christ (e.g., I Thessalonians 4:4).

The Holy Scriptures

God promised the good news through the Hebrew prophets: "Which He promised before through His prophets in the Holy Scriptures" (Romans 1:2). (See Hebrews 1:1.) This does not mean the Hebrew prophets consciously foretold the coming of the church, in which distinctions between Jews and Gentiles are erased (Ephesians 3:1-6; Galatians 3:28; Colossians 3:11; Romans 10:12). The church was a mystery not revealed to the prophets of the Old Testament era. (See Ephesians 2:11-22; 3:1-6, especially 3:4-5.) Although the Hebrew Scriptures foretold the salvation of Gentiles, the prophets did not see that salvation occurring through an obliteration of the distinction between Jews and Gentiles. The salvation of Gentiles foretold in the Hebrew Scriptures will yet occur during Daniel's seventieth week (the Great Tribulation) and the Millennium as Gentiles come to faith in the Jewish Messiah through the influence of the redeemed nation of Israel. (See Isaiah 9:1-2; 11:6-10; 42:1-7; 49:1-

6; 54:1-3; 60:1-16; 66:19; Malachi 1:11; Romans 11:11; Revelation 7:4-17; 20:3. "Nations" is a reference to the Gentile nations of the world as opposed to the nation of Israel.

The Scriptures gain their holy status by their association with God Himself through inspiration. (See II Timothy 3:16; II Peter 1:20-21.) The written revelation of God had its beginnings with Moses in about 1500 B.C. On Sinai, God Himself wrote the Ten Commandments in tables of stone, and He also gave Moses a great deal more to write down. (See Exodus 17:14; 24:4, 7; 34:27-28; Numbers 33:2; Deuteronomy 31:9, 22, 24-26; John 5:45-47; Luke 16:31; 24:44.)

Like Moses, Joshua himself wrote the words of God (Joshua 24:26). God used many other holy men to communicate His revelation to His people. (See Hebrews 1:1.) These included Samuel, David, Solomon, Isaiah, Joel, Amos, Jonah, Micah, Hosea, Jeremiah, Nahum, Habakkuk, Zephaniah, Ezekiel, Daniel, Obadiah, Haggai, Zechariah, Ezra, Nehemiah, Malachi, and others.

All together, the Old Testament says, "Thus saith the LORD" about 2,500 times. Similar phrases abound, like "And God said," and "The word of the LORD came unto me, saying . . ." The internal witness of the Old Testament is that it is the very Word of God, and it contains warnings against tampering with the text. (See Deuteronomy 4:2; Proverbs 30:5-6.)

The Hebrew Scriptures in use during Jesus' life on earth were the same as our Old Testament today. The only difference is the order of the books and the division of some of them. Originally, books like I and II Kings were one book, and the last book in the Hebrew Bible is our I and II Chronicles. The present order and division of some books originated with the Septuagint, a Greek translation of the Hebrew Scriptures accomplished during the third century B.C.

Since Jesus used the same Hebrew Scriptures we do, and since He was God Himself, His statements about the trustworthiness of the Hebrew Bible are extremely important. They assure us of the reliability of our Old Testament. Jesus endorsed the Pentateuch (the first five books of the Bible) (Mark 12:26). He declared that Moses wrote about Him (John 5:39, 45-47). Jesus affirmed that David wrote psalms (Mark 12:36; Luke 20:41-44) and Daniel wrote the book bearing his name (Matthew 24:15).

The Hebrew Bible is divided into three sections: (1) the Law (Genesis, Exodus, Leviticus, Numbers, and Deuteronomy); (2) the Prophets (Joshua, Judges, I and II Samuel, I and II Kings, Isaiah, Jeremiah, Ezekiel, and the twelve smaller books from Hosea to Malachi); (3) the Writings (Psalms, Proverbs, Job, Song of Solomon, Ruth, Lamentations, Ecclesiastes, Esther, Daniel, Ezra, Nehemiah, and I and II Chronicles). Jesus gave His divine endorsement to each of these sections (Luke 24:44). (See also Matthew 7:12; Luke 16:31.) He assigned infallibility to all of these Old Testament books when He said, "All things must be fulfilled" (Luke 24:44). He recognized these were not the writings of mere men, but of men inspired and moved by the Holy Spirit.

Since the New Testament was not written until after the ascension of Jesus, can we look to Him for endorsement of any New Testament writings? Yes, Jesus gave advance testimony concerning the integrity of the New Testament: "I have yet many things to say unto you, but ye cannot bear them now. Howbeit when he, the Spirit of truth, is come, he will guide you into all truth: for he shall not speak of himself; but whatsoever he shall hear, that shall he speak: and he will shew you things to come" (John 16:12-13, KJV). "But the Comforter, which is the Holy Ghost, whom the Father will send in my name, he shall teach you all things, and bring all things to your remembrance, whatsoever I have said unto you" (John 14:26, KJV).

Jesus approved the writings of His apostles and disciples in advance: (1) He had many more things to say, but His followers were not ready to hear them. (2) The Spirit of Truth, yet to come, would guide them into *all* truth. In other words, there would be no error in what He directed them to write. (3) The Spirit of Truth is not independent of God, but speaks the voice of God. (4) The Spirit of Truth would reveal future events, i.e. prophecy, to them. (5) The disciples would be supernaturally empowered by the Holy Ghost to remember everything Jesus had said.

As indicated by the fifth point above, the words that Jesus had spoken would form an indivisible part of the Scriptures to be written after His ascension. He claimed that His words were the words of God, inspired, infallible, and inerrant: "He who rejects Me, and does not receive My words, has that which judges him—the word that I have spoken will judge him in the last day" (John 12:48). "The words that I speak to you are spirit, and they are life" (John 6:63). "Heaven and earth will pass away, but My words will by no means pass away" (Matthew 24:35).

The testimony of Jesus is that both the Old and New Testaments were divinely inspired, that they are actually the words of God, and that their preservation is more sure than that of the universe itself.

The doctrine of inspiration finds its primary expression in II Timothy 3:16: "All Scripture is given by inspiration of God." The word "inspiration" comes from the Greek *theopneustos*, which in its most literal sense means "God-breathed." This word suggests the accuracy of the evangelical position of verbal, plenary inspiration. That is, since Scripture is made up of words, the inspiration is verbal. It extends to the very words of Scripture. Since the inspiration extends to *all* Scripture, the inspiration is plenary (full).

Inspiration occurred in the context of the Holy Spirit moving holy men to write in such a way that the words they wrote accurately expressed the mind of God (II Peter 1:20-21). The process was not one of mechanical dictation, for God did not override the personalities, cultural backgrounds, vocabularies, or writing styles of these men. And yet we can truly call what they wrote "the Word of God," for God influenced them to write in such a way that every word was perfectly suited to communicate His message. Inspiration does not mean that every statement in the Bible is a statement of truth, for the Scripture records the erroneous words of Satan and unregenerated people. But inspiration does mean that everything the Bible reports, even from Satan and unregenerated people, is accurately reported.

The apostle Peter pointed out that the ultimate authority is the *written* Word, rather than any external manifestation that is subject to interpretation by the human senses: "There came such a voice to him from the excellent glory. . . . And this voice which came from heaven we heard. . . . We have also a more sure word of prophecy. . . . The scripture . . . came not in old time by the will of man: but holy men of God spake as they were moved by the Holy Ghost" (II Peter 1:17-21, KJV).

This passage refers to the audible voice that spoke from heaven in approval of Jesus, but we have a more sure word than that: the Scripture, written by holy men carried along by the Holy Ghost. The audible voice was subject to the human sense of hearing; there could have been disagreement as to what was actually said. The written Word, the Scripture, is sure. There should be no debate about the actual words written, though there may, of course, be debate as to their meaning.

It is entirely appropriate to refer to the Scriptures as "holy." God gave them through holy men, and they communicate a holy message.

Called to Be Saints

Paul concluded his salutation, "To all who are in Rome, beloved of God, called to be saints . . ." (Romans 1:7). Thus he identified the recipients of his letter. He wrote to all the believers in Rome. They were God's beloved, and they were called saints. The word "saints" is translated from *hagios*, which means "holy ones."

This word, a form of which is translated "sanctify," has to do primarily with separation. The Hebrew background of the word (*qadosh*) describes first the way God Himself is separate from His creation, then the way His chosen people, the Jews, are separated from the nations around them by the law of Moses.

Only by association did the word begin to take on implications of morality. When we think of the word "holy," we immediately think of the moral aspects of the word. But in a way this misses the point. A person could be a strict, uncompromising moralist, but if he had no faith in God he would not be holy. Because we have faith in God, we *are* holy; our faith separates us from the unbelieving world around us. Genuine faith will produce results, and these results include morality. But it is not the morality that makes us holy; it is the faith.

The Greek text reads "called saints" or "called holy." The translators have supplied the words "to be," which could imply that believers are called to *become* saints, or to become holy. But the scriptural text itself declares that the believers in Rome *are* saints because they are "the called of Jesus Christ" (Romans 1:6). (See also Romans 8:27; 12:13; 15:25-26, 31; 16:2.)

The Holy Spirit

Several times the letter to Rome refers to the Holy Spirit. One such example is Romans 5:5: "Now hope does not disappoint, because the love of God has been poured out in our hearts by the Holy Spirit who was given to us." (See also Romans 9:1; 14:17; 15:13, 16.) By definition, the Spirit of God is holy, since God is holy. (See Leviticus 11:44-45; Luke 1:35.)

The radical monotheism of Scripture does not allow us to think of God in a fragmented way, although we know Him as Father, as the Son of God in the Incarnation, and as the Holy Spirit. In general, it seems appropriate to think of God in His transcendence as Father. To be transcendent means God is above and beyond His creation; He is prior to and greater even than the Incarnation. This in no way diminishes the significance of the Incarnation: Jesus Christ was and is fully God; every aspect of the essence of deity dwells bodily in Him (Colossians 2:9).

But even when He was manifest in genuine and complete human nature (I Timothy 3:16; John 1:14), God was still omnipresent, omniscient, and omnipotent. Although, in the Incarnation, God willingly accepted the limitations of human existence, He still existed above and beyond those limitations.

The Son of God is God incarnate, or manifest in the flesh. Jesus is the image of the invisible God (Colossians 1:15; II Corinthians 4:4; Hebrews 1:3). He is God made known in human existence. (See John 1:18; 8:19; 14:6-11.)

The Holy Spirit is God in His immanence. That God is with us means He is immanent; He is not only above and beyond us, nor is He manifest only in the human existence that today is exalted to the right hand of the Majesty on high (Hebrews 1:3). God is also with us and among us and in us through His Holy Spirit. (See, e.g., Romans 14:17; 15:13, 16; I Corinthians 6:19; 12:3; II Corinthians 13:14.)

There is no thought in Scripture of God as "persons." There is one God who is in essence Spirit (John 4:24). He eternally dwells in the realm above and beyond His creation (Psalm 8:1; 57:5, 11; 68:33; 96:5; 108:5; 113:4; Isaiah 57:15), He is manifest in flesh in the person of Jesus Christ (I Timothy 3:16), and He lives and works and moves in His creation and among His people by the presence of His Holy Spirit (Acts 17:27-28).

Sanctification Is by Union with Christ

Although the Greek *hagios* does not appear in Romans 6 and the noun form *hagiasmos* appears only twice, sanctification is the theme of the chapter. Beginning with a description of the new birth (verses 1-10), at which point God grants positional sanctification to the believer, the chapter moves to a discussion of the process of yielding oneself to God on a continuing basis, which is progressive sanctification (verses 11-23).

Sanctification has to do with separation. But before it is separation *from* something, it is separation *unto* something. The idea of separation *from* is a consequence of separation *unto*. Specifically, separation *from* sin is a consequence of separation *unto* God.

The point is that sanctification is not merely a matter of nonconformity to the lifestyles or values of those about us. There are many people, including those in non-Christian religions, who for a variety of reasons do not conform to the lifestyles or values of prevailing culture. This does not mean they have experienced biblical sanctification.

Biblical sanctification occurs only as believers identify with the true God and accept the manner of life and values commended in Scripture as normative. This separation *unto* God of necessity results in separation *from* non-Christian lifestyles and values. As a culture increasingly distances itself from faith in the true God and conformity to His Word, those who do have faith in Him and endeavor to live by biblical precepts will experience a greater degree of separation from the world. This does not happen so much because of changes in the body of believers, but because of changes in society at large.

Sanctification is sometimes called holiness. It involves increasing conformity to the character of Christ, which should be evident in the life of each believer as he grows in grace and in the knowledge of the Lord and Savior, Jesus Christ. (See II Peter 3:18.) There is a sense in which sanctification occurs simultaneously with justification, but there is also a sense in which it is progressive. (See I Corinthians 6:11; Hebrews 10:14.) The positional sanctification we experience in conjunction with regeneration is to be worked out or lived out in our daily life. (See Philippians 2:12-13.)

The doctrine of soteriology includes conversion, justification, regeneration, sanctification, calling, repentance, faith, adoption, glorification, and union with Christ. The last relates to our intimate relationship with the Lord Jesus and the effect of His life upon us. (See II Corinthians 5:17; Ephesians 1:3-4; 2:10; I Thessalonians 4:16; I Corinthians 15:22; Colossians 1:27; Galatians 2:20; John 15:4-5.)

Not only are believers "in Christ," they also identify with Him in His suffering (Romans 8:17), His crucifixion (Galatians 2:20), His death (Colossians 2:20), His burial (Romans 6:4), His resurrection (Ephesians 2:5; Colossians 3:1), and His glorification and inheritance (Romans 8:17).

The implications of this union include the following: First, we are accounted righteous (Romans 8:1). Second, we live in the strength of Christ (Philippians 4:13). Third, we will suffer for our identification with Christ (Mark 10:39; John 15:20; Philippians 3:8-10; I Peter 4:13). Last, we will reign with Christ (Luke 22:30; II Timothy 2:12).

Romans 6 indicates that the believer's sanctification—his separation unto God and from sin—occurs as a consequence of the believer's identification with Jesus Christ in His death and burial. Because the believer has identified with Jesus in His death and burial, he is also identified with Him in His resurrection, and thus in life, or in freedom from the domination of the sin nature.

The "sin" of Romans 6 is not so much specific acts of sin but the sin nature to which all are enslaved until they are set free from its control by the new birth. The freedom from sin described in this chapter is not immunity from temptation or failure, but release from enslavement to the sin principle.

Romans 6:1 asks, "What shall we say then? Shall we continue in sin that grace may abound?" Since grace overwhelms sin (Romans 5:20), it may seem reasonable from a human standpoint to encourage people to sin all the more so grace could be even more abundant. But any reader who thinks this has missed the point. The reason for the abundance of grace is not to doom people to slavery to sin so that the grace of God will stand out in even greater contrast, but rather to release people from slavery to sin. Grace abounds not merely to demonstrate the depravity of sin, but to assure that no matter how deep one may be in the pit of sin, grace can reach farther down.

Romans 6:2 answers the question: "Certainly not! How shall we who died to sin live any longer in it?" It resorts to the strongest possible denial, *me genoito*, which can be literally translated, "May it never be!" The idea that we should sin even more profusely in order to give grace an opportunity to abound even more is thus rejected.

The purpose of this question is not to condemn those readers who may have been falling short of God's glory, but simply to state that those who have died to sin can no longer live under its domination. Death means separation.[2] This passage does not mean that sin is extinct for the believer, that he can no longer be tempted or that he can no longer yield to temptation. What it means is that the believer has been separated from sin's ruling power. (See verse 7.)

If believers have died (aorist tense, indicating an action completed in the past) to sin, they can no longer draw from sin as the source of their life. Though a believer may be tempted and may succumb to a specific temptation, sin is no longer his way of life. Whereas prior to his regeneration the believer sinned as a way of life and thought little or nothing of it, the believer who sins senses that his sin has an aura of death about it, and he has a desire to confess his sin to God and to be cleansed from the effects of sin. Since sin's ruling power over him is broken, the believer can no longer live in sin.

Romans 6:3 begins a discussion of the practical aspects of the believer's death to sin: "Or do you not know that as many of us as were baptized into Christ Jesus were baptized into His death?" Although the context does not mention water, there seems little doubt verses 3-4 refer to water baptism. Where Holy Spirit baptism is unquestionably in view, we find something other than identification with Jesus Christ in His death and burial: "For by one Spirit we were all baptized into one body— whether Jews or Greeks, whether slaves or free—and have all been made to drink into one Spirit" (I Corinthians 12:13). Spirit baptism identifies the believer with the body of believers, the church; water baptism identifies the believer with the person of Jesus Christ in His death and burial. Spirit baptism is a baptism from which the believer is never raised, for if he were raised, he would be disassociated from the body of believers, the church.

Water baptism is a baptism from which the believer *is* raised. This does not mean the believer is no longer identified with Jesus Christ, but that, having been identified with Jesus in His death and burial, he is now identified with Him in His resurrection.

Since the baptism discussed in Romans 6:3-4 is not the same as that of I Corinthians 12:13, and since I Corinthians 12:13 has to do with Spirit baptism, the baptism of Romans 6:3-4 must be water baptism. This idea finds support in that water baptism is always in the name of Jesus, to identify the believer with Jesus Christ in His death and burial. (See also Acts 2:38; 8:16; 10:48; 19:5; I Corinthians 1:13; 10:2; Galatians 3:27; I Peter 3:21.)

We must not confuse the believer's "dying out to sin," which is part of the process of sanctification, with the believer's identification with Jesus Christ in *His* death, which is part of conversion. No matter how devout a believer may be, he could never "die out to sin" so completely and thoroughly that he would merit salvation. Salvation is a gift of God made possible not by the believer's devotion or success in sanctification, but by the work of Jesus Christ on the believer's behalf. The only hope a believer has for salvation—and the only hope he needs—is to be identified with Jesus Christ in His death, burial, and resurrection.

It is sometimes said that a believer "dies out to sin" in repentance. In the context of Romans 6:2-4, however, the death to sin experienced by the believer occurs when the believer not only repents but is baptized to unite with Christ Jesus in His death. Repentance is necessary for salvation, but, in addition to confession of sins, repentance includes a radical reorienting of one's thoughts (about

186

God, life, and sin), values, and purposes. Though at repentance a believer confesses his sins and declares his intention to turn away from them, he does not have within himself the moral strength to keep this commitment permanently. The removal of sin's dominating power comes, not by a person's ability to repent, but by the death of Christ on the believer's behalf, and the way the repentant believer identifies with Christ in His death is by water baptism.

The significance of the name of Jesus Christ in water baptism is not merely the verbal formula, although the name of Jesus must be called over the baptismal candidate. The verbal formula is made necessary by baptism's purpose: the identification of the baptismal candidate with the person of Jesus Christ in His death and burial. We are baptized in the name of Jesus Christ because baptism unites us with Jesus in His death and burial.

Water baptism identifies us with Jesus Christ in His death so we may subsequently be identified with Jesus in His life: "Therefore we are buried with Him through baptism into death, that just as Christ was raised from the dead by the glory of the Father, even so we also should walk in newness of life. For if we have been united together in the likeness of His death, certainly we also shall be in the likeness of His resurrection" (Romans 6:4-5). The "newness of life" in which we walk contrasts with the spiritual death we experienced before our regeneration. Previously we were separated from fellowship with God (a state of spiritual death), but now we are united with God by His Spirit (a state of spiritual life).

Christ's resurrection came by the "glory of the Father," meaning that the power of God caused it. Glory is a synonym for the power of God at work. (See Psalm 63:2; Matthew 6:13; Ephesians 1:19-20; Colossians 2:12; Jude 25; Revelation 5:13.) The "power" of God and the "glory" of God are also terms for the "Spirit" of God. (See Luke 1:35; Romans 1:4; 8:11.) Just as certainly as the Holy Spirit raised Jesus Christ from the dead, so the same Spirit will enable the believer who has been united with Christ in His death to live in fellowship with God. (See Romans 8:11.) Verse 5 may allude to the bodily resurrection of the believer, but the context indicates that the more direct reference is to the spiritual life the believer experiences as a consequence of his identification with Christ in His death.

Romans 6:6-7 further discusses our identification with Jesus Christ in His death: "Knowing this, that our old man was crucified with Him, that the body of sin might be done away with, that we should no longer be slaves of sin. For he who has died has been freed from sin." The "old man" is the sin nature or sin principle that dwells in everyone as a consequence of Adam's sin. (See Ephesians 4:22; Colossians 3:9.) It is not necessary for believers to experience physical crucifixion as Jesus did; His death was on our behalf. But the believer must be identified with Jesus in His crucifixion or death. As verses 3-4 have just pointed out, this occurs at water baptism. Thus baptism, when received in faith and repentance, is much more than a public profession of one's desire to follow Christ. It actually accomplishes the crucifixion or death of the sin nature; it does away with the "body of sin."

The death of the old man does not mean the believer no longer has the sin nature indwelling him (I John 1:8) or that he can no longer be tempted, for death does not mean extinction. It means separation. When we identify with Jesus Christ in His death, the ruling power of sin over us is broken, so that "we should no longer be slaves to sin." The human body without the human spirit is dead (James 2:26), but the human body is not extinct simply because of its separation from the human spirit. It still exists and can be acted upon, although it cannot act. In a similar way, the sin nature, the "body of sin," is not extinct because it is dead. And although it is incapable of dominating the believer's life, the believer can still act upon it by yielding his members as instruments of unrighteousness unto sin (verses 12-13).

It may seem strange at first to think that anyone who is free from domination by the sin nature would yield to sin, but that is precisely what Adam and Eve did in the Garden of Eden. Temptation to sin does not arise merely from the sin nature, but from the power of choice inherent in being human. Certainly the sin nature enhances temptation and tilts a person more decidedly toward sin, but a person can be tempted on the basis of the power of choice alone. Jesus was tempted, yet He certainly did not possess a sin nature. (See Hebrews 4:15.)

The unbeliever is a slave to sin; he has no power to break free from it. (See verses 17-20.) The baptized, Spirit-filled believer has been set free from sin's controlling power; he has the ability, by the power of the Holy Spirit, to resist temptation. (See verses 12-14, 18.) As Romans 6:7 puts it, "He who has died has been freed from sin." Identification with Jesus Christ in His death and resurrection frees the believer from sin's control.

Romans 6:8 restates a truth presented in verses 4-5: "Now if we died with Christ, we believe that we shall also live with Him." Identification with Jesus Christ in His death results in identification with Jesus Christ in His life. As in verse 5, there may be an ultimate reference here to the bodily resurrection of the believer and to eternal life in the presence of God, but the immediate and contextual concern is apparently for the believer's life on earth.

The difference between the resurrection of Christ and the resurrection of all others recorded in Scripture is that every other person raised from the dead experienced death a second time. Jesus did not. His resurrection was final; He will never die again: "Knowing that Christ, having been raised from the dead, dies no more. Death no longer has dominion over Him" (Romans 8:9). In this sense He is the "firstborn" and "firstfruits" from the dead. (See I Corinthians 15:20; Colossians 1:18.)

The latter part of verse 9 uses an expression that explains the relationship of sin to the believer after the believer's identification with Christ in His death: "Death no longer has dominion over Him." Just as death has no more power over Christ, so the sin nature has no more power over the believer. It can control him no longer.

The death of Jesus was "to sin": "For the death that he died, He died to sin once for all; but the life that He lives, He lives to God" (Romans 6:10). As we noted about verse 2, we must not confuse "dying out to sin" with the believer's identification with Jesus Christ in His death. The same grammatical structure appears in both verses 2 and 10. The believer does not duplicate in his own life Jesus' death "to sin," for this occurred when Jesus died on the cross. The only way the believer can experience this is by the marvel of his union with Christ in water baptism (verses 3-4).

Jesus had no sin nature to which to die. Grammatically, His death "to sin" means His death *in reference to* sin. In other words, Jesus died because of the sin problem; He died as an offering for sin. (See Isaiah 53:10; II Corinthians 5:21.) Those who identify with Jesus Christ in His death *in reference to* sin enjoy freedom from sin's control just as Jesus enjoys freedom from death.

The death of Jesus "to sin" was "once for all." (See Hebrews 7:27; 10:10.) No further work is needed to free believers from sin's controlling power. Not only is there no need for a continual reenactment of the death of Jesus, as in some religious traditions, but also there is no need for human efforts to earn release from the power of sin. We can add nothing to complete the work Christ did to free people from sin's power; we need only to apply His work to our lives.

Indeed, Christ's work was more than sufficient. (The Hebrew word translated "offering" in Isaiah 53:10 means an offering that is more than required.) The freedom from sin we find in the death of Christ must be *applied* in each believer's life, but it does not need to be *supplemented* by feeble human efforts to conquer temptation. Temptation will always be present during this life, but we find victory over specific temptations by relying on the work of Christ on Calvary, not by resorting to techniques and formulas in an attempt to divert temptation or weaken its force.

The resurrection life Jesus now lives is "to God." It is life *in reference to God,* or on account of or because of God. Jesus was resurrected "by the glory of the Father" (see comments on verse 4), so His life is testimony to the reality of God, just as His death was testimony to the reality of sin.

Just as Jesus died to sin and now lives to God, so the believer should "reckon," or count himself, to be truly dead to sin but alive to God: "Likewise you also, reckon yourselves to be dead indeed to sin, but alive to God in Christ Jesus our Lord" (Romans 6:11). This is not a matter of mental gymnastics, but an alignment of one's thoughts with the reality of identification with Jesus Christ in His death, burial, and resurrection. Since the believer is free from the ruling power of sin, he should agree with that truth and rely upon its consequences. When the believer sets himself in agreement with the facts of his identification with Christ, he can boldly confront temptations to sin like the victor over sin that he is.

The life "to God" the believer enjoys is "in Christ Jesus our Lord." Romans thus reminds us again that all the blessings we enjoy arise from our union with Christ.

Since the believer has been set free from sin's ruling power, he can now refuse to allow sin to reign, even though he is still in his "mortal body": "Therefore do not let sin reign in your mortal body, that you should obey it in its lusts" (Romans 6:12). This passage does not suggest that any believer, during his life on this earth, will reach a point of sinless perfection. (See I John 1:8; Romans 3:23.) But by virtue of the believer's union with Christ, the believer can refuse to let sin *rule* him, or *reign* over him (like a king). The only person over whom sin reigns is the person who surrenders completely to sin. The command of this verse—"Therefore do not let sin reign in your mortal body"—could never be given to a person who had not been identified with Jesus Christ in His death, burial, and resurrection. The unregenerate person would find it quite hopeless to keep such a command.

But the command is not wasted on those who are in union with Christ; they really do have the ability to refuse sin's attempt to rule them.

The latter part of this verse offers insight into sin's method of operation: "That you should obey it *in its lusts*." The word "lust" means "strong desire," and the word can be used in a negative or positive way. (See Galatians 5:17.) The lusts of sins are "sinful passions" (Romans 7:5). Temptation first creates within a person a strong desire for forbidden behavior; this method of operation is as old as Genesis 3.

When the believer understands that wrong desires no longer belong to him, but belong to sin, he will be helped in resisting temptation. In other words, temptation itself is not sin. The lusts themselves do not belong to the believer who is in union with Christ, but to sin itself. If a believer thinks temptation is sin, and that he could not be tempted if he had not already sinned, he will more quickly succumb to temptation. But if he recognizes temptation for what it is—sin's attempt to bring him under its control—he will more readily resist it.

We are not to lend our "members" to sinful purposes, but we are to let them be used for right purposes: "And do not present your members as instruments of unrighteousness to sin, but present yourselves to God as being alive from the dead, and your members as instruments of righteousness to God" (Romans 6:13). The "members" include any part of a human being's resources over which he has control. This includes the physical body, but it also includes the mind and other aspects of the immaterial person. We are to present our members to God on the basis of the spiritual life that sprang from identification with Jesus in His death.

The believer's union with Christ results in the destruction of sin's dominion: "For sin shall not have dominion over you, for you are not under law but under grace" (Romans 6:14). The issue here is not temptation or even the commission of specific acts of sin. The issue is whether sin rules the believer. For those who were under the law of Moses as the rule of life, the law itself served to arouse sinful passions (Romans 7:5). One purpose of the law was to make sin exceedingly sinful (Romans 7:13). That is, the law illustrated the helplessness of man to free himself from sin's dominion by merely trying to adhere to high codes of conduct. If believers were under the law of Moses, sin would have dominion over them. But since they are under grace, sin's ruling power is broken. The law demanded perfect obedience and thereby heightened the sin problem, whereas grace gives the believer both the desire and the ability to do what is right. (See Philippians 2:13; I Corinthians 15:10.)

Romans 6:15 asks another question similar to that in verse 1: "What then? Shall we sin because we are not under law but under grace? Certainly not!" Does freedom from the law of Moses mean the believer should abandon himself to sin? The answer is, "May it never be" (Greek, *me genoito*).

The reason believers are not to engage in sin is because in yielding themselves to sin they become sin's slave all over again: "Do you not know that to whom you present yourselves slaves to obey, you are that one's slaves whom you obey, whether of sin to death, or of obedience to righteousness?" (Romans 6:16). If believers persist in serving the sin nature, they will eventually suffer death—separation from fellowship with God—all over again. If, on the other hand, believers yield themselves to obey the leading of the Holy Spirit to do what is right, they become slaves of right living.

Believers are to be grateful for the release from captivity to sin that comes from the "form of doctrine" or teaching inherent in the gospel of Jesus Christ: "But God be thanked that though you were slaves of sin, yet you obeyed from the heart that form of doctrine to which you were delivered" (Romans 6:17). This statement apparently refers back to the theme of the book in Romans 1:16-17. When a person from his heart (sincerely) places his faith and trust exclusively in Jesus Christ for his salvation, he sets in motion a chain of events that results in his release from slavery to sin. The Roman believers had experienced this wonderful deliverance. Their identification with Christ was so complete it could be said that they were delivered to the teaching of justification by faith.

Though the believers in Rome struggled with human imperfections, as demonstrated by the tensions between the Jewish and Gentile believers, they had in fact "been set free from sin" and "became slaves of righteousness" (Romans 6:18). This does not mean they were free from temptation, but that they were free from sin's power to control or rule them. They could now resist sin's attempts to dominate them.

Using human reasoning to communicate this point to the immature Romans, the inspired Paul encouraged them to present all their resources in service of right living just as they had previously presented them in service of wrong living: "I speak in human terms because of the weakness of your flesh. For just as you presented your members as slaves of uncleanness, and of lawlessness leading to more lawlessness, so now present your members as slaves of righteousness for holiness" (Romans 6:19). The wrong living in which they had previously engaged had no point of termination: it tended to expand into ever increasing lawlessness. "Uncleanness" here is moral impurity. Sin is never satisfied. The sin to which a person yields soon loses its ability to satisfy, so that increasing depravity results. (See Romans 1:21-32.) But when a believer surrenders his members in service of right living, holiness results. This, the production of holiness, is the ultimate end of sanctification. By definition, holiness is identification with the character of God in His moral perfections.

Before a person becomes a believer, when he is still a slave to the sin nature, he is completely "free" from right standing with God: "For when you were slaves of sin, you were free in regard to righteousness" (Romans 6:20). This does not mean a sinner is as wicked or perverse as he could possibly be, but it does mean that apart from union with Christ there is no right standing with God. An unregenerate person may be relatively moral, but morality is not righteousness in the eyes of God. Only by identifying with Jesus Christ in His death, burial, and resurrection can we find genuine righteousness.

Service to the sin nature yields no life-giving fruit. It produces only death, or separation from fellowship with God: "What fruit did you have then in the things of which you are now ashamed? For the end of those things is death" (Romans 6:21). Paul knew his readers were ashamed of their previous life as sin's slaves.

By contrast, those who are set free from sin's controlling power by virtue of their union with Christ, and who have become the servants of God, enjoy the life-giving fruit of their behavior: "But now having been set free from sin, and having become slaves of God, you have your fruit to holiness, and the end, everlasting life" (Romans 6:22). In this life, right choices result in holiness (verse 19); ultimately, right choices result in eternal life. No one earns salvation by good works, but the genuine faith that saves believers results in right actions.

Sin results in separation from God: "For the wages of sin is death, but the gift of God is eternal life in Christ Jesus our Lord" (Romans 6:23). Union with Christ results in eternal life. The spiritual death resulting from sin is the "wages" of sin. In other words, the sinner receives the just payment for his actions. (See Revelation 20:12-13.) He will have no basis to complain about God's judgment, for it will be based exclusively on what the sinner has done. But the eternal life that comes from union with Christ is a "gift." It is not deserved, earned, merited, or worked for. It is a gift that results in right living; it is not a reward for right living.

The Law Is Holy

It may seem strange that in a passage discussing the way the law of Moses arouses sinful passions (Romans 7:5), the book would say, "There the law is holy, and the commandment holy and just and good" (Romans 7:12). But the law was holy because of its association with the holy God. It is holy in the same sense that the Scriptures are holy. (See Romans 1:2.) This statement does not imply that the law of Moses is binding on new covenant believers.

Holy Branches

In a discussion of the relationship between the root of the Abrahamic covenant and the branches, which were Abraham's descendants through Sarah, Romans 11:16 says, "For if the firstfruit is holy, the lump is also holy; and if the root is holy, so are the branches." This passage offers two illustrations to demonstrate the same point. The first illustration is from Numbers 15:20. Israel was to "offer up a cake of the first of [their] ground meal as a heave offering." As an offering to the Lord, this cake was holy. If the part of the dough offered as the firstfruit was holy, then the whole batch of dough was holy. Likewise, since a tree springs from its root, if the root is holy, the entire tree, including the branches, is holy.

In short, the origin of a thing determines the character of all that springs from it. In this case, the "firstfruit" or the "root" of national Israel is Abraham. (See Romans 4:1.) Since Abraham was holy, all his offspring through the promised seed (Romans 9:7-13) were holy as well. The word "holy" does not necessarily imply moral excellence here, but God's sovereign setting apart of national Israel for special treatment because of their identification with their father Abraham.

A Holy Sacrifice

As the Book of Romans begins its discussion of practical Christianity, it focuses on the need for believers to dedicate their lives to God without reservation (Romans 12:1), to resist the temptation to conform to the values of the present age (Romans 12:2), to identify and minister in the specific areas of their spiritual giftedness (Romans 12:3-8), to conduct themselves in a Christ-like way both inside and outside the fellowship of the church (Romans 12:9-21).

Previously, this letter has specifically addressed Jewish believers (Romans 2:17) and Gentile believers (Romans 11:13). Now it views the church as a whole; ethnic distinctions are of no significance in what it has to say. It is concerned only with "brethren" who, regardless of their ethnic heritage, must equally dedicate themselves to God's service: "I beseech you therefore, brethren, by the mercies of God, that you present your bodies a living sacrifice, holy, acceptable to God, which is your reasonable service" (Romans 12:1).

The appeal is based on "the mercies of God" as described in the previous eleven chapters of the letter. The preposition *dia*, translated "by," has the idea "by means of." The appeal is not by the mercies of God; the appeal is for believers to dedicate themselves to God by means of His mercies. (See Romans 9:15-16, 18, 23; 11:30-32.) The word "therefore" ties this appeal to all that has gone before; the appeal is meaningful only in the context of the mercies that God has extended to both Gentiles and Jews. If salvation were by works and not by faith (see Romans 3:27; 11:6), this appeal would be pointless; the readers would have earned their salvation by their performance and nothing more could be asked of them. But since salvation is, by the mercy of God, based on faith and not works, Christians—although saved—still need to bring their actions into conformity with their profession.

Christians need to present their bodies to God as "a living sacrifice." The word translated "present" is translated "yield" in Romans 6:13, 16, 19. This word reminds us of the earlier exhortation; now that we have been united with Christ in His death, burial, and resurrection, it remains our responsibility to consistently "yield" the members of our bodies to God's service. Here, Romans depicts the entire body, not just its various members, as a candidate for surrender to God. The exhortation is positive not negative; the focus is on what the believer is to do with his body rather than what he should not do with it.

The word "bodies" reminds us of the Jewish sacrificial system, but the Hebrews viewed man as an integrated whole, not fragmented into separate parts. They were a visceral people; they spoke of mental activity and emotions as tied to the inner organs of the body. For example, the Hebrew word translated "reins" in the KJV means "kidneys." (See Job 16:13; 19:27; Psalm 7:9; 16:7; 26:2; 73:21; 139:13; Proverbs 23:16; Isaiah 11:5; Jeremiah 11:20; 12:2; 17:10; 20:12; Lamentations 3:13.) In Jewish thought, the kidneys were the seat of the character, affections, and emotions. The liver was identified with anger. (See Lamentations 2:11). The heart was equated with the will. (See, e.g., Deuteronomy 6:5; Psalm 119:2; Proverbs 3:5; Ecclesiastes 8:11.) This concept appears also in the New Testament in such phrases as "bowels of compassion" (I John 3:17, KJV). The Greek word translated "bowels," *splangchna*, is accurately translated; it means "intestines."

All of this illustrates that to the Jews there was no split between mind and body. Western anthropology is strongly influenced by Greek philosophy, which tends to view the body as evil and man as a spirit imprisoned in a body. But Jewish anthropology views man as a whole. For example, though God formed Adam's body of the dust of the ground, as God breathed the breath of life into his nostrils he became "a living soul" (Genesis 2:7). When the God of Israel declares, "All souls are mine" (Ezekiel 18:4), He does not mean just that the immaterial part of man belongs to Him, but that man in his totality—all that makes man, man—belongs to Him. Eight souls were saved in Noah's ark; this means, of course, eight people (I Peter 3:20). There certainly are both material and immaterial components to human existence (Hebrews 4:12; I Thessalonians 5:23), but from the perspective of the Hebrews, to speak of any component is to address the whole of man. The Hebrews were aware of the distinction between the material and immaterial components of human existence, but they tended to think of human existence in a holistic way. Abraham asked Sarah to say she was his sister, so his "soul" could live (Genesis 12:13, KJV). The NKJV rightly translates, "That I may live." Throughout the Hebrew Scriptures, "soul" is a metaphor for "person." (See, for example, Exodus 12:15, 19; 31:14; Leviticus 4:2; 5:1, 2, 4, etc.)

The Hebrew Scriptures frequently use "body" to refer to the material part of a person who is dead (e.g., Leviticus 21:11), or to refer to one's reproductive abilities (e.g., Deuteronomy 28:4), but since Romans 12:1 describes a *living* sacrifice rather than a dead one and since it certainly has no reference to physical reproduction, here "body" represents "the totality of one's life and activities, of which [the] body is the vehicle of expression."[3] Thus the appeal here is not just for Christians to present their immaterial component to God, but for them to surrender their entire being to His service. The reference to the "mind" in verse 2 demonstrates this point.

Thus, the challenge is to present *ourselves*, not just our material part, to God. The new covenant idea of sacrifice is radically different from that of the old covenant. There is no longer any need for priests to offer sacrifices for sin; Christ finished that work once and for all (Hebrews 9:26; 10:12, 18). Instead, the New Testament priests offer spiritual sacrifices (I Peter 2:5), namely praise and thanksgiving (Hebrews 13:15; Philippians 4:18), doing good and giving to those in need (Hebrews 13:16), themselves (Romans 12:1; Philippians 2:17), and the results of evangelistic efforts, new converts (Romans 15:16). None of these sacrifices are salvific; the only redemptive sacrifice is that of Jesus Christ. The sacrifices of the new covenant are responses of gratitude for the mercies of God.

God considers the sacrifice of one's self to Him to be holy (set apart unto God and thus from sin) and pleasing ("acceptable"). This is the believer's "reasonable service." The word translated "reasonable" (*logiken*) has to do with one's rational powers. It comes from *logos*, which means "word" or "reason." Thus the sacrifice is not that of a body alone, but of the full scope of human existence, including the powers of reason.

This word anticipates the appeal in verse 2: "Be transformed by the renewing of your mind." Service offered to God is not mindless; it does not require (and God does not accept) "service" that comes from an abandonment of one's God-given ability to think and reason. The person who puts his mind fully in God's service worships Him as surely as the person who gives God his hands and feet. (See Mark 12:30.) The word translated "service" (*latreian*) has to do with any ministry or service rendered to God.

A Holy Kiss

Toward the end of his letter, Paul wrote, "Greet one another with a holy kiss" (Romans 16:16). This is one of four times Paul recommended that believers greet one another with a holy kiss. (See I Corinthians 16:20; II Corinthians 13:12; I Thessalonians 5:26.) It was customary among Christians in the first century to greet one another this way, just as it is today in Western society to greet one another with a handshake: "The holy kiss . . . was primarily a symbolic expression of the love, forgiveness, and unity which should exist among Christians. As such, it became associated with the celebration of the Lord's Supper as a prelude to its observance."[4]

The emphasis is not so much on the kiss itself as on the greeting being "holy." This admonition was appropriate to a church that struggled with tension between ethnic groups. No doubt, out of sheer social convention, the believers in Rome were greeting one another with a kiss; Paul's concern was that they greet one another with the awareness of their mutual separation unto God and in the fear of God. Since the focus is on the holiness of the greeting and not making the form of the greeting itself normative for all time, it does not follow that believers in cultures where kissing is not a socially acceptable form of greeting are obliged to practice it. In other cultures, believers can use the normative cultural greeting, but whatever it is, it should be "holy."

Notes

[1]Surprisingly enough, the KJV translates a form of *qadosh* with the word "sodomite" and "sodomites" in Deuteronomy 23:17; I Kings 14:24; 15:12; 22:46; and II Kings 23:7. During the darkness of Israel's sin, morally perverted individuals served as temple prostitutes when the Temple in Jerusalem was corrupted for the worship of false gods. They are called *qadesh* because they were separated from society at large for Temple service, depraved though it was.

[2]Scripturally, death is not extinction, but separation. Charles Ryrie points out: (1) Physical death is the separation of body from spirit (James 2:26). (2) Spiritual death is the separation of a person from God (Ephesians 2:1). (3) The second death is eternal separation from God (Revelation 20:14). (4) Death to sin is separation from the ruling power of sin in one's life (Romans 6:14). (See C. C. Ryrie, *The Ryrie Study Bible*, King James Version (Chicago: Moody Press, 1978), 1602.

[3]Walvoord and Zuck, 487. See also Frank E. Gaebelein, ed., *The Expositor's Bible Commentary* (Grand Rapids, MI: Zondervan Publishing House, 1976) 10:127.

[4]John F. Walvoord and Roy B. Zuck, eds., *The Bible Knowledge Commentary*, New Testament Edition (Wheaton, IL: Victor Books, 1983), 548.

Jews:
Showing the Favor of God
To His National People

The church at Rome was composed of both Gentile and Jewish believers. Tension already existed between Jewish and Gentile communities in the city because many Romans had converted to Judaism. During the A.D. 40s, the Roman emperor Claudius forced all Jewish people to leave the city. (See Acts 18:2.) Thus, until Claudius's death, the church in Rome was made exclusively of Gentile believers. Thereafter, Jewish Christians returned to Rome. (See Romans 16:3.) The tensions between the Jewish and Gentile communities at large reached into the church, prompting the discussion in this letter about reconciliation and mutual appreciation and acceptance.[1]

Apparently some Jewish believers were quick to condemn Gentiles for their sins, though they themselves were equally guilty. (See Romans 2:1.) Though advanced revelation is a wonderful gift from God, the sinfulness of the heart of man prompts him to use the superior revelation he has received as a cause for pride, arrogance, and judgmentalism of those who have received lesser revelation. It would be better for those who have received greater revelation to remember that with greater knowledge comes greater responsibility. (See James 3:1.)

Since the law enabled the Jews to define sin clearly (see Romans 7:7), they tended to be quick to judge the obvious sinfulness of the Gentile nations. But by doing so, they were judging themselves, for they were guilty of the same sins. Since the Jews had advanced revelation, they had no excuse either for their sinfulness or for their judgmentalism of others.

Experience has shown that when a person seems consumed with condemning people who practice specific sins, it is often because he struggles with those same sins himself. His condemnation of others is actually the outworking of his self-condemnation. This does not mean we should not oppose sin. But the safest ground for the preacher is to declare the whole counsel of God rather than to focus only on one expression of human sinfulness. If a person finds himself obsessed with fighting a narrow range of sin, he should prayerfully ask God to search his heart. (See Psalm 19:12.) Though he may not be practicing the specific sin he compulsively condemns, he may be struggling with the same root sin that gives birth to a particular sinful practice.

According to I John 2:16, there are three root sins: pride, greed, and moral impurity. Thus, though the person who repeatedly and harshly condemns riches may not be rich, he may be greedy. The person who is consumed with condemning sexual sins may not actually be participating in them, but he may struggle with impure fantasies and desires. In the Sermon on the Mount, Jesus pointed out that not only is adultery a sin, but so is lust (Matthew 5:27-28). Since we tend to be most sensitive to our own faults when we see them in others, we should always examine ourselves for the sins we condemn.

The Gentile believers in Rome were apparently somewhat antagonistic toward the Jewish believers, as indicated by their boasting and reveling in their freedom from the law of Moses (Romans 11:13, 18, 20, 25; 14-15). The Jews were also critical of the Gentiles (Romans 2:17-29; 3:9).

We see the arrogance of some Jewish believers in that they were so confident that they were qualified to guide the "blind," that they were a light to those in darkness, that they were able to instruct the "foolish" and "babes" (all referring to Gentile believers). (See Romans 2:19-20.) The reason for their sense of superiority was that they were the recipients of superior revelation. The Gentiles had only general revelation (creation and conscience, Romans 1:18-20; 2:14-16); the Jews had the law, which imparted knowledge and truth.

In spite of its rebuke of Jewish believers for their misguided sense of superiority over Gentile believers, Romans reveals that national Israel retains a place of destiny in the future plans of God. (See Romans 9-11.) When the purposes of God for this present age are complete, He will turn again to national Israel to perform every unfulfilled unconditional promise He has made to them. (See Romans 11:26-29.)

The words used to identify Jewish believers in this letter include "Jew," "Jews," "Israel," and "circumcision."

To the Jew First

The phrase "the Jew first" appears three times in the letter to the church at Rome: "For I am not ashamed of the gospel of Christ, for it is the power of God to salvation for everyone who believes, for the Jew first and also for the Greek" (Romans 1:16); "Tribulation and anguish, on every soul of man who does evil, of the Jew first and also of the Greek; but glory, honor, and peace to everyone who works what is good, to the Jew first and also to the Greek" (Romans 2:9-10).

This phrase does not imply ethnic superiority of Jews over non-Jews. Historically, the gospel of Christ was offered first to the Jewish people, then to the Gentiles. Since the Roman Empire was strongly influenced by Greek culture, the Jewish people considered all non-Jews as "Greeks." When the spiritual leaders of the Jews rejected Jesus, He turned to the Gentiles to offer Himself to them as the fulfillment of the Hebrew prophecies that the Jewish Messiah would also bring salvation to the Gentiles. (See Matthew 12:14-50.) Salvation under the new covenant is still available to the Jewish people, but it is now available to all—Jew and Gentile—who will believe. (See Galatians 3:28; Colossians 3:11.)

Just as the Jewish people had priority in revelation, so they have priority in judgment. Greater revelation brings greater responsibility. But this priority in judgment also means that they have priority in receiving glory, honor, and peace if they do what is right.

Jewish Boasting

Addressing Jewish believers directly, Romans 2:17 says, "Indeed you are called a Jew, and rest on the law, and make your boast in God." The Jewish members of the Roman church apparently insisted on retaining their ethnic identity, using it as a claim to superiority over the Gentile believers. The Greek word translated "rest" in this verse appears elsewhere only in Luke 10:6. It describes stopping to lean on something to be supported and held up by it. These Jewish believers continued to trust in the law of Moses rather than advancing on to embrace the new covenant exclusively. Since the Gentile believers did not adhere to the law of Moses, these Jews made this an issue of boasting. (See Romans 3:27.)

The Inward Jew

Romans 2:25-27 explains that circumcision is of no spiritual benefit if a person does not obey the law of Moses completely and that Gentiles who keep the requirements of the law will stand in judgment against circumcised Jews who did not.[2] Then Romans 2:28-29 points out, "For he is not a Jew who is one outwardly, nor is that circumcision which is outward in the flesh; but he is a Jew who is one inwardly; and circumcision is that of the heart, in the Spirit, and not in the letter; whose praise is not from men but from God."

A misunderstanding of these two verses has led some to think that, given the proper circumstances, Gentiles can become "spiritual Jews" or "spiritual Israel." That is not the point, and neither term ever appears in Scripture. This passage provides an example of a Hebraism. First-century Jewish readers would have understood the meaning as follows: "For he is not a Jew who is one *only* outwardly, nor is circumcision that which is *only* outward in the flesh; but he is a Jew who is one *also* inwardly; and circumcision is that *also* of the heart." The passage does not deny that a

Jew is ethnically Jewish or that a circumcised man is actually circumcised. Rather, it tells Jews that their physical lineage, descent from Abraham, and physical conformity to the commandment of circumcision (which their parents actually chose for them when they were eight days old) did not make them right with God or deserving of God's commendation. The only thing that would bring them God's approval was if they were spiritually alive. (See John 3:5-6.) If they were not "in the Spirit" (Romans 8:9), outward conformity was of no value in gaining favor with God.

The Jew's Advantage

The demonstration of the equal sinfulness of the Jews and the Gentiles prompted Jewish readers to ask, "What advantage then has the Jew, or what is the profit of circumcision?" (Romans 3:1). It may be difficult for Gentiles to understand how shocking chapter 2 would have been to Jewish believers reading this letter for the first time. The Jews had for centuries gloried in being God's chosen people, in being the direct descendants of the patriarchs Abraham, Isaac, and Jacob. They looked to Moses as their chief prophet and to the law he received at Sinai as the supreme revelation of God. They focussed their devotion on the Temple in Jerusalem, to them the most sacred spot on earth. To the Jews, circumcision was a physical sign that they were special people to God; it summed up all facets of their religious life. For this reason the term "uncircumcised" came to be a kind of shorthand way of referring with disdain to various Gentiles. (See Judges 14:3; I Samuel 17:26, 36; Isaiah 52:1; Jeremiah 9:25-26.)

But Romans informs Jewish readers that, given the right circumstances, uncircumcised Gentiles can be as pleasing to God as Jews. Nothing in the law of Moses prepared the Jews for this concept. They knew their Hebrew Scriptures prophesied of the coming salvation of Gentiles, but these Scriptures described this salvation as occurring in conjunction with the exaltation of the nation of Israel, which had not transpired when Paul wrote this letter. Indeed, the salvation of Gentiles predicted in the Hebrew Scriptures would occur through the influence of the redeemed nation of Israel. (See Psalm 2:6-8; 22:27-31; 24:1-10; Isaiah 1:2-3; 11:1, 10-13; 42:1, 6; 49:6, 22; 54:3; 60:3, 5, 11-12, 16; 61:6, 9; 62:2; 66:12; Jeremiah 16:19; 23:5-8; 30:7-11; Ezekiel 20:33-40; 37:21-25; Zechariah 9:10; 14:16-19; Malachi 1:11.) But to first-century Jewish readers, Romans no doubt seemed to dismiss cavalierly one of the most important aspects of the Jewish religion. The question in Romans 3:1 anticipates their indignant response: "Paul, if what you are saying is true, what value is there to being Jewish, or to being circumcised?"

Under divine inspiration, Paul responded to the anticipated question of his Jewish readers by declaring there are many advantages to being Jewish and thus to participating in circumcision: "Much in every way!" (Romans 3:2a). But the only advantage specifically listed at this point is this: "Chiefly because to them were committed the oracles [Scriptures] of God" (Romans 3:2b). Later the letter lists several other advantages (Romans 9:4-5). But it is significant that none of the advantages make the Jews better people than the Gentiles. The only difference mentioned here between the Jews and the Gentiles is that the Jews received greater revelation (the oracles or written Scriptures) and thus had greater responsibility. It was indeed an advantage to have greater revelation, but as a whole the Jews had not responded to this advantage by fulfilling the requirements of the revelation given to them.

Jews Are No Better Than Gentiles

As a Jew himself, Paul asked, "What then? Are we better than they? Not at all. For we have previously charged both Jews and Greeks that they are all under sin" (Romans 3:9). Apparently some Jewish readers of Paul's letter believed they were morally or ethnically superior to Gentiles because God had chosen them for advanced revelation. In fact, God chose the nation of Israel to receive advanced revelation not because of their moral or ethnic superiority, but in spite of their sinfulness. (See Galatians 3:19.) In order for Jews to claim superiority over the Gentiles, they would have to live in complete obedience to the law of Moses. Since they did not, they had no room to judge others who were not completely obedient to lesser revelation.

The God of the Jews Is the God of the Gentiles

Since the law of Moses does not impart moral or spiritual superiority to Israel, nor does it indicate that God relates to them exclusively, Romans asks if only the Jews have a claim on God: "Or is He the God of the Jews only? Is He not also the God of the Gentiles? Yes, of the Gentiles also" (Romans 3:29). God is as much the God of the Gentiles as of the Jews, even though Gentiles historically received lesser revelation (general revelation).

As an example, the God of Israel sent a Hebrew prophet, Jonah, to a Gentile city, Nineveh. God was just as concerned about Nineveh as about Israel. And He extended forgiveness to Nineveh simply on the basis of their repentance, with no hint that He required these Gentiles to adhere to the law of Moses. The important lesson for Jewish readers was that superior revelation did not hint that they were superior people in any way; it simply meant they had greater responsibility.

Circumcised or Uncircumcised: Justification Is by Faith

In a statement sure to startle Jewish readers, Romans 3:30 declares, "There is one God who will justify the circumcised by faith and the uncircumcised through faith." Justification—right standing with God—comes on the basis of faith in Christ Jesus, regardless of one's ethnic origin.

A Blessing Exclusively for Jews?

Romans 4:7-8 quotes Psalm 32:1-2 to demonstrate David's grasp of justification by faith: "Blessed are those whose lawless deeds are forgiven, and whose sins are covered; blessed is the man to whom the LORD shall not impute sin." Then Romans 4:9 asks, "Does this blessedness then come upon the circumcised only, or upon the uncircumcised also?" The word "circumcised" refers to the Jews; Gentiles are the "uncircumcised." It would have been no problem for Jewish readers to believe David's description of the blessedness, or the happy state, of the Jewish people whose sins were covered and to whose records the Lord did not count sin. But could the uncircumcised Gentiles enjoy the same privilege?

Was Abraham Righteous Before He Was Circumcised?

No doubt surprisingly to Jewish readers, Romans 4:9b-10 points out that Abraham was granted right standing with God before he was circumcised: "For we say that faith was accounted to Abraham for righteousness. How then was it accounted? While he was circumcised, or uncircumcised? Not while circumcised, but while uncircumcised." The only thing that preceded Abraham's justification was his faith. (See verse 3.)

Abraham: First the Father of Gentile Believers

If Abraham was counted righteous before he was circumcised, what was the point of circumcision? "And he received the sign of circumcision, a seal of the righteousness of the faith which he had while still uncircumcised, that he might be the father of all those who believe, though they are uncircumcised, that righteousness might be imputed to them also" (Romans 4:11). No doubt it sounded incredible to the Jews in Rome when they first read these words, but the reason God justified Abraham prior to his circumcision was so he could be the father, not just of the circumcised Jews, but also of the uncircumcised Gentiles. In fact, he was the father of Gentile believers before he was the father of Jewish believers. (See Galatians 3:29.)

Walking in Abraham's Steps

God later required circumcision of Abraham so that he could also be the father of the Jewish people, for God knew He would require circumcision of Israel under the law of Moses: "And the father of circumcision to those who not only are of the circumcision, but who also walk in the steps of the faith which our father Abraham had while still uncircumcised" (Romans 4:12).

But for the Jew, it is not sufficient that he be circumcised; he must also "walk in the steps of the faith" Abraham possessed even before he was circumcised. Of course, to be counted righteous, Gentiles must also walk in the same steps of faith demonstrated by Abraham. All people approach God in the same way: by faith. The Jews must do everything the Gentiles do, and in addition they must be circumcised.

This discussion refers to the old covenant, for under the new covenant Jews do not need to be circumcised. When the old covenant was binding upon Israel, any Gentiles who were saved were saved by faith in the true God. If they wished, Gentiles could convert to the Jewish religion, but even then they still had to have genuine faith in the true God in order to be saved.

Israel's Past, Present, and Future

A major portion of Romans—three entire chapters— is taken up with an examination of national Israel's past, present, and future. This discussion is no doubt made necessary by the repeated assertion of the termination of the law of Moses (Romans 3:20-22, 27-28; 7:4-6; 8:3) and the inability of ethnic Jewishness to grant special standing in relation to salvation (Romans 2:11-13, 17-29; 3:9-19, 29-30; 4:9-15; 5:20; 7:5, 8, 10-11, 14). It seems reasonable to think that at this point first-century Jewish readers would ask if the heritage they had long valued was of any real significance.

On the other hand, first-century Gentile readers may have felt strengthened in libertarian boasting (Romans 11:17-24) by the rebuke of their Jewish brethren's sense of moral superiority (Romans 2:1-24; 3:9-19).

The three chapters now in view (9-11) serve to

restore the sense of destiny that national Israel had deservedly held for many centuries. Although national Israel, who had been elected by God, was now under His divine disapproval, their future restoration in His eyes was assured.

Paul's Intense Concern for the Salvation of Jews

Paul's poignant words communicate well the depth of his love for his people: "I tell the truth in Christ, I am not lying, my conscience also bearing me witness in the Holy Spirit, that I have great sorrow and continual grief in my heart. For I could wish that I myself were accursed from Christ for my brethren, my kinsmen according to the flesh" (Romans 9:1-3).

Paul invoked his own conscience as a witness of the truthfulness of his assertion here. (Compare Romans 1:9.) Paul was "in Christ" (see Romans 6:3-8 and 8:1), and to be "in Christ" was by definition to be "in the Spirit." (See Romans 8:2, 9-10.) The Holy Spirit was dwelling within him and offered no condemnation of his sincerity or truthfulness in conjunction with his confession, as dramatic as it was.[3]

Paul expressed his "great sorrow" and "continual grief" and even his willingness—if it would help—to wish himself "accursed from Christ for [his] brethren, [his] kinsmen according to the flesh." Why did Paul think it necessary to preface these expressions with such a strong affirmation of his truthfulness? No doubt it was because of the radical nature of the previous comments about the termination of the law of Moses and the inability of the Jews' ethnic heritage to grant them special standing in matters of salvation. It is possible some could have accused Paul of anti-Semitism. If there were those who slandered him on another subject (see Romans 3:8), it is not difficult to imagine that some would have done so on this point. By his solemn words, Paul reinforced the sincerity of his claims in these verses.

Even though the Pauline Epistles frequently reaffirm the passing of the law of Moses and the inability of one's Jewish heritage to grant him special favor in the eyes of God (e.g., Galatians 3:10-18; 5:3; Philippians 3:1-9), Paul was still deeply concerned about the spiritual well-being of his fellow Jews. It is doubtful that we can fully appreciate the intensity of his emotional pain expressed in his willingness to be "accursed from Christ" if it would bring salvation to his brethren. Perhaps his feeling corresponds to the rare event described by Jesus wherein someone is willing to lay down his life for his friends (John 15:13).

Advantages of Being Jewish

Romans 3:1 anticipates the question, "What advantage then has the Jew, or what is the profit of circumcision?" The answer is, "Much in every way!" but the only advantage mentioned in the immediate context is, "Because to them were committed the oracles of God" (Romans 3:2). Romans 9:4-5 extends the list of the advantages to the heritage of Israel: "Who are Israelites, to whom pertain the adoption, the glory, the covenants, the giving of the law, the service of God, and the promises; of whom are the fathers and from whom, according to the flesh, Christ came, who is over all, the eternally blessed God. Amen." In addition to the Hebrew Scriptures, Israel's blessings included the following:

1. *The adoption.* God commanded Moses to inform Pharaoh, "Thus says the LORD: 'Israel is My son, My first-

born'" (Exodus 4:22). This statement came prior to the law of Moses, and it indicates God's unconditional election of the nation for special treatment and revelation. The adoption of national Israel was, however, on a different basis and for a different purpose than the adoption of those who are born of the Spirit under the new covenant. (See Romans 8:15, 23.) The adoption of Israel was a national adoption without regard for individual faith; even those within national Israel who were not people of faith enjoyed certain nonsalvific, corporate benefits. (See Deuteronomy 4:31, 37; 9:5.)

2. *The glory.* This phrase refers to the Shekinah, the visible glory of God that appeared to Israel on various occasions. (See Exodus 16:10; 24:17; 40:34; I Kings 8:11.) Since the Shekinah was the glory of God, it came to represent God Himself to the Jewish people. Thus Jewish readers would have understood Romans 3:23 ("All have sinned and fall short of the glory of God") to mean that all fail to measure up to the standard of perfection exemplified by God Himself. When James 2:1 says that Jesus Christ is the "Lord of glory," it means Jesus is the visible manifestation of the invisible God. (See Hebrews 1:3.)

3. *The covenants.* We can identify eight covenants in Scripture: (a) *the Edenic covenant* (Genesis 1:28-31; 2:8-17); (b) *the Adamic covenant* (Genesis 3:14-19); (c) *the Noahic covenant* (Genesis 9:1-29); (d) *the Abrahamic covenant* (Genesis 12:1-4; 13:14-17; 15:1-18; 17:1-8); (e) *the Mosaic covenant* (Exodus 20); (f) *the Palestinian covenant* (Deuteronomy 27-30); (g) *the Davidic covenant* (II Samuel 7:8-17); and (h) *the new covenant* (Jeremiah 31:31; Hebrews 8:6-13; Matthew 26:27-28). Of these, five pertain specifically to Israel: the Abrahamic,

Mosaic, Palestinian, Davidic, and new covenants.

4. *The giving of the law*. The law of Moses was such a preeminent covenant and so unique in its purpose that Romans considers it separately here.[4] (See Deuteronomy 5:1-22.)

5. *The service of God*. This phrase relates to service in the Tabernacle and Temple worship. It has to do exclusively with Israel, for it springs from the law of Moses.

6. *The promises*. God gave many promises to ancient Israel, the chief of which was the coming of the Messiah. (See Isaiah 7:14; 9:6-7; 11:1-10; 42:1-4; 61:1-3.)

7. *The fathers*. Further blessings to national Israel included the origin of the nation from the highly revered fathers: Abraham, Isaac,and Jacob. These three men are so significant in Scripture that God identified Himself by their names. (See Exodus 3:6, 15-16; 4:5; Matthew 22:32; Mark 12:26; Luke 20:37; Acts 3:13; 7:32.)

8. *The Messiah*. The final, and thus ultimate, blessing national Israel enjoyed was the coming of the Messiah and His receiving His humanity through the nation of Israel. Here we find one of the strongest possible claims of the Messiah's deity: He is the supreme ("over all"), eternally blessed God.

This section concludes, as it began, with a solemn affirmation of truth. Here it is, "Amen." "Amen" is the English transliteration of the Greek transliteration of the Hebrew word, which means something like, "So be it!"

Paul had now set aside, for the sincere reader of his letter, any question as to his deep personal concern for national Israel. Although the law of Moses has terminated and Israel possesses no salvific advantage, God still has a special concern for Israel.

All Who Are of Israel Are Not Israel

Romans 9:6 reiterates the statement in Romans 3:3 that the unbelief of some of national Israel does not negate the faithfulness of God: "But it is not that the word of God has taken no effect. For they are not all Israel who are of Israel." Though many individual Israelites rejected their Messiah, not all did. The latter part of the verse restates another fact previously introduced: ethnic Jewishness was not enough to identify a person as a genuine Israelite. (See 2:28-29; 4:11-12; Galatians 3:6-7; John 8:37-39.) Even the Old Testament identified the genuine Israelite as the person who not only received his physical lineage from Abraham, but who also had a clean heart (Psalm 73:1). The "Israel of God" in Galatians 6:16 no doubt includes only those Jews who embrace Jesus as the Messiah.

The identification of genuine Israel as those Jews who believe helps us interpret Romans 11:26: "And so all Israel will be saved." This does not mean a time is coming when every ethnic Jew will automatically be saved, but a great revival is coming to Israel, and every ethnic Jew who puts his faith in Jesus the Messiah will be saved.

The Promised Seed

Romans 9:7-8 embarks on an elaborate illustration of the point that physical Jewishness is not sufficient to make a person a genuine Jew: "Nor are they all children because they are the seed of Abraham; but, 'In Isaac your seed shall be called.' That is, those who are the children of the flesh, these are not the children of God; but the children of the promise are counted as the seed." Not all of the offspring of Abraham are part of ethnic Israel. The promised seed came through one specific son of Abraham: Isaac. Abraham had other sons, including Ishmael, Zimran, Jokshan, Medan, Midian, Ishbak, and Shuah (Genesis 16:1-16; 25:1-2), but none of these was the promised seed. Thus, God Himself made a distinction among Abraham's offspring.

The promise of God that gave birth to national Israel was that Abraham would have a son born of Sarah, not of Hagar or Keturah or any other woman: "For this is the word of promise: 'At this time I will come and Sarah shall have a son'" (Romans 9:9). (See Genesis 18:10; Hebrews 11:11.)

The route of the promised seed became even more specific with each generation: "And not only this, but when Rebecca also had conceived by one man, even by our father Isaac (for the children not yet being born, nor having done any good or evil, that the purpose of God according to election might stand, not of works but of Him who calls), it was said to her, 'The older shall serve the younger'" (Romans 9:10-12). Isaac, the promised seed of Abraham, fathered twins by his wife Rebecca. Through whom would the promised seed come? Both? Further demonstrating that ethnic heritage alone does not identify a person as a genuine Israelite, even before Esau and Jacob were born, before either of them had done good or evil, God said to Rebecca, "The older shall serve the younger." (See Genesis 25:23.) The promised seed came through one of the twins, the younger one, Jacob. It is possible, therefore, for a person to be the offspring of Abraham and even of Isaac, and still not be an Israelite.

The Purpose of God According to Election

God made the choice of Jacob over Esau so "that the purpose of God according to election might stand, not of works but of Him who calls." God did not predestine Esau to forfeit his birthright, but in His foreknowledge (see Romans 8:29), He knew the choices Esau would make. God's statement that "the older shall serve the younger" was not a sentence of judgment on Esau even before he was born, but a simple fact: Because of the choices Esau would make, he would forfeit his privileges as the firstborn son.

We must understand the phrase "the purpose of God according to election" to refer contextually to "the election of grace" (Romans 11:5). In His sovereign will, God has determined to elect those who respond to His grace. It is the grace of God that works to give right desires and right abilities. (See John 15:5; I Corinthians 15:10; Philippians 2:13.)

God extended His grace to Esau, but he chose an immoral and profane lifestyle and disregarded his birthright. (See Hebrews 12:15-17.) God, knowing Esau would do this, declared to Rebecca, "The older shall serve the younger." This election is not according to works; things done by the influence and enablement of God's grace are not "works" in which anyone can boast. (See Ephesians 2:8-10.) Works done by the power of the flesh in an effort to gain favor with God are not a cause for election. (See Romans 3:27; 4:2-5.) Romans does not dispute, however, that genuine faith will produce tangible results. (See James 2:21-26.)

If Esau and Jacob had been capable of doing good or evil in their mother's womb, and if on that basis God had made His decision as to whom He would elect, the election would have been of works. Both boys had the same father and the same mother; in fact, they were twins. Theoretically, either could have been the one God chose to advance the Abrahamic lineage. Both were sinners, and God extended His grace to both. But Esau rejected the grace of God, while Jacob received it. (See Hebrews 11:21.)

The inability of Esau and Jacob to do good or evil in the womb demonstrates that unborn children are not sinners. They do possess the fallen Adamic nature, the sin principle (see Romans 5:12), and as they grow up they will sin, but at birth they are innocent. (See Romans 7:9.)

Romans 9:13 quotes from Malachi 1:2-3 to demonstrate further that the promised seed came through Jacob, not Esau, and that not all of Isaac's descendants are counted in national Israel: "As it is written, 'Jacob I have loved, but Esau I have hated'" (Romans 9:13). We should note that God did not make this statement before they were born. In the context of Malachi, Jacob represents national Israel, and Esau represents national Edom.

Moreover, we must understand the words "love" and "hate" according to their use in the Hebrew language. The Hebrew language has no equivalent for many English words expressing lesser degrees of love, like fondness, affection, tenderness, or liking. In the Hebrew language, a person is either loved or hated. There is no middle ground. The Hebrews experienced the same range of emotions as any other people, but their language had no way to express varying degrees of love. There was no equivalent to the Greek *agape, phileo*, and *eros*. As with many other words, only the context can define the meaning of love and hatred in the Hebrew Scriptures. God's "hatred" of Esau was not the extreme hatred of the English word, for even with Esau's failure, God promised him and his descendants special blessings. (See Genesis 27:38-40.) In essence, Malachi 1:2-3 means that God chose national Israel instead of Edom.

The Mercy and Compassion of God

Here Romans anticipates that its readers may question the righteousness (right actions) of God in view of His rejection of Esau and acceptance of Jacob: "What shall we say then? Is there unrighteousness with God? Certainly not!" (Romans 9:14). Since Esau and Jacob were both innocent in their mother's womb, was it wrong for God to say, "The older shall serve the younger"? Romans again uses the strong *me genoito* to deny the possibility that God's decision was unjust. The only way anyone could accuse God of unrighteousness would be if the tables had been turned, and Esau had responded to the grace of God rather than Jacob, and still God had rejected Esau.

Romans 9:15 quotes from God's statement to Moses following Israel's idolatry while Moses was first on Mount Sinai receiving the tables of stone: "For He says to Moses, 'I will have mercy on whomever I will have mercy, and I will have compassion on whomever I will have compassion.'" (See Exodus 33:19.) The context in Exodus indicates that God does not arbitrarily extend His mercy and compassion to some—without regard to their faith or their desire to know Him—and withhold it from others on the same basis. God had showed His mercy and compassion for Israel in delivering them from Egyptian captivity, and He continued to demonstrate mercy even after their idolatry by inviting Moses back up on Sinai to receive another set of the stone tables. God is not erratic in sometimes showing mercy on people of faith and sometimes withholding it, or sometimes extending mercy to disobedient people and sometimes withholding it. God is consistently merciful; He extends mercy even to the disobedient. From a human standpoint, it seems God would *not* have continued to show mercy to Israel after their idolatry. But God alone will decide how long to extend mercy.

Favor with God is not achieved by human effort; it is a result of God's merciful nature: "So then it is not of him who wills, nor of him who runs, but of God who shows mercy" (Romans 9:16). This is reminiscent of John's statement, "But as many as received Him, to them He gave the right to become children of God, even to those who believe in His name: who were born, not of blood, nor of the will of the flesh, nor of the will of man, but of God" (John 1:12-13). People do not become the children of God by human effort, nor are they predestined to be saved before they are born. To become the children of God, people must *believe in His name*. Believing is not a meritorious work, because it is God who gives everyone the ability to believe in His name. (See II Peter 3:9; John 3:16.)

Although salvation arises from "God who shows mercy," people are still responsible to receive it. But no one can ever say he is saved because of his own effort; salvation is a direct result of the mercy of God. If an Esau rejects the mercy of God and thus loses his privileges, he cannot fault God for not showing mercy. If a Jacob receives the mercy of God and thus gains privileges, he cannot boast that he has been rewarded for his works; he is simply the recipient of God's mercy.

The Sovereignty of God

To further illustrate God's sovereignty in showing mercy and compassion, Romans 9:17 quotes Exodus 9:16, where Moses declared the words of God to Pharaoh: "For this purpose I have raised you up, that I may show

My power in you, and that My name may be declared in all the earth." We must not too readily jump to the conclusion that God raised up Pharaoh purposefully to hold him up to ridicule before all the earth through the ten plagues and the destruction of the Egyptian army in the Red Sea. God could have showed His power and declared His name by Pharaoh's willing release of the Israelites at Moses' first request.

The first request Moses and Aaron made to Pharaoh to let the people of Israel go was a sincere request. Pharaoh had the freedom to respond positively to that request. Even when he rejected the first request, Moses and Aaron again pleaded with him to allow the Israelites to go three days' journey into the desert. (See Exodus 5:1-3.) God did not predestine Pharaoh to refuse the request, or the request itself would have been meaningless. The point of this historical account is that God showed mercy even to Pharaoh; it was God Himself who raised Pharaoh up, and His intention was to demonstrate His power and to declare His name through Pharaoh. When Pharaoh rejected the request of Moses and Aaron, God's intention to show His power and to declare His name did not change, but the way He accomplished these purposes did change.

The situation with Pharaoh demonstrates that God is sovereign in showing mercy on some and in hardening others: "Therefore He has mercy on whom He wills, and whom He wills He hardens" (Romans 9:18). This does not mean that God refuses to show any mercy at all on some, but that He alone determines when to stop showing mercy and when to harden the hearts of those who reject His mercy. It is true that God hardened Pharaoh's heart. (See Exodus

9:12; 10:1, 20, 27; 11:10; 14:8.) It is also true that God told Moses and Aaron that He would harden Pharaoh's heart (Exodus 7:3). But before God actually hardened Pharaoh's heart, Pharaoh hardened his own heart. (See Exodus 8:15, 32.) Twice before Scripture says that God hardened Pharaoh's heart, it says simply that Pharaoh's heart was hardened. (See Exodus 7:14; 9:12.) Although the KJV translates Exodus 7:13, "And he hardened Pharaoh's heart," the NKJV translates it, "And Pharaoh's heart grew hard." When we examine the entire context, it seems that Pharaoh first hardened his heart against God and that God subsequently further hardened Pharaoh's heart. I Samuel 6:6 records that both the Egyptians and Pharaoh hardened their own hearts. Though God at first extended mercy to Pharaoh by requesting him to release the people of Israel, Pharaoh rejected the appeal and hardened his heart. Shortly, God determined the time for mercy was past and He further hardened Pharaoh's heart.

Romans 9:19 anticipates that readers will ask, "Why does He still find fault? For who has resisted His will?" This question is similar to Romans 3:5, and it is the result of human reasoning. If God knows in advance what decisions a human being will make, and if He makes pronouncements in advance as to what those decisions will be—as He did with both Esau and Pharaoh—and if He even goes so far as to say what He will do as a result of human decisions, and if He does not continue to show mercy on some as long as on others, does this not indicate that people are merely puppets or robots who cannot help what they do? How can God find fault with people and hold them personally responsible under such circumstances?

If the doctrine of unconditional election were true, this

would be a valid objection. All people would do exactly what they were predestined to do, and it would be valid to ask how God could find fault with anyone. But those who would ask this question misunderstand the difference between foreknowledge and predestination. (See Romans 8:29.) Romans 8 is the contextual background of the present discussion, and its detailed explanation of foreknowledge, predestination, calling, justification, and glorification probably addressed a specific deficiency in the understanding of the Roman believers. Indeed, the initial purpose of the discussion in chapter 9 is to restore to the Roman believers the hope for which Paul could not commend them.[5] It is difficult to see how the doctrine of unconditional election (predestination) could restore hope; it contributes to a sense of hopelessness, for there is always the possibility that an individual is not included in the elect.

Romans 9:20-21 rebukes anyone who would question the sovereignty and mercy of God: "But indeed, O man, who are you to reply against God? Will the thing formed say to him who formed it, 'Why have you made me like this?' Does not the potter have power over the clay, from the same lump to make one vessel for honor and another for dishonor?" Human beings should no more question the work God is doing in their lives than the clay should question the potter. A potter can use a lump of clay to make either an exquisite vessel designed for honored use or a plain utilitarian vessel. He does not consult the clay about the type of vessel it wants to be, but in both cases he makes a useful vessel. The question here is not whether the potter makes anything of the clay; the question is what *type* of vessel he makes.

Based on the analogy of the clay and the potter,

Romans 9:22-23 points out that God in some cases may wish to show His wrath and make His power known: "What if God, wanting to show His wrath and to make His power known, endured with much longsuffering the vessels of wrath prepared for destruction, and that He might make known the riches of His glory on the vessels of mercy, which He had prepared beforehand for glory?" Even then, however, He endures "with much longsuffering the vessels of wrath prepared for destruction." After God has endured the hardness of people with "much longsuffering," He can—if He wishes—show His wrath and His power in any way He pleases. These "vessels of wrath" are "prepared for destruction," not by being predestined to destruction but by their own rejection of the mercies of God.

On the other hand, God makes known the riches of His glory "on the vessels of mercy, which He had prepared beforehand for glory." God does not predestine some for mercy and ultimately for glory (see Romans 8:18, 21), but He showers His riches on those who respond to His grace. He foreknew what their response to His grace would be, so He determined in advance, based on His foreknowledge, to glorify them. This is the exact parallel of Romans 8:29-30.

The "vessels of mercy" are those "whom He called, not of the Jews only, but also of the Gentiles" (Romans 9:24). We can understand the reference to being "called" in one of two ways. First, it may simply mean that God calls both Jews and Gentiles to salvation, without suggesting that He calls only select ones and fails to call others. Obviously, God has called all who come to Christ, but this does not mean He called no one except those who came. Second, it may refer to the calling of Romans 8:28-

29, which is a call to those who are already saved to be conformed to the image of God's Son.

The Remnant Will Be Saved

Romans 9:27-28 quotes Isaiah 10:22-23 from the Septuagint: "Isaiah also cries out concerning Israel: 'Though the number of the children of Israel be as the sand of the sea, the remnant will be saved. For He will finish the work and cut it short in righteousness, because the LORD will make a short work upon the earth.'" Verse 27 serves to explain verse 6 further. The number of the children of Israel was as the sand of the sea—so far as national Israel was concerned—but only a remnant would be saved. This remnant is the true Israel. (See Romans 11:26.) It will be made up of those who respond in faith to the mercies of God. (See Hebrews 11:6.) When the time comes to accomplish this work, God will do it quickly. This passage apparently describes the work the Holy Spirit will do in national Israel during the time of Jacob's trouble, the Great Tribulation. (See Revelation 7:3-8.)

Again, Romans 9:29 quotes from the Septuagint: "And as Isaiah said before: 'Unless the LORD of Sabaoth had left us a seed, we would have become like Sodom, and we would have been made like Gomorrah.'" (See Isaiah 1:9.) Except the Lord of Hosts (angels) had preserved a remnant in Israel, the nation would have been totally destroyed like Sodom and Gomorrah. Instead of supporting unconditional election and predestination apart from foreknowledge, this verse supports the idea that God continued to show mercy upon Israel even in the nation's darkest night of spiritual deadness. Because He continued to extend His mercy to them, some responded in faith and thus the nation was preserved. We should remember that even Sodom and Gomorrah would have been spared if there had been as few as ten righteous people, and we do not know what God's response to Abraham would have been if Abraham had asked for an even lower number. (See Genesis 18:20-33.)

Israel's Present Rejection

In view of God's sovereign election of the nation of Israel (Romans 9:1-29), it would seem reasonable to ask why the nation was not enjoying the favor of God at the time of the writing of this letter. The next section of the letter (Romans 9:30-10:21) is a response to that question. The reason national Israel was experiencing God's rejection is that they had rejected the Messiah, Jesus Christ.

Because national Israel pursued right standing with God by the works of the law and not by faith in God, the nation stumbled over Jesus. They could not bring themselves to believe that one Man could do for them and on their behalf what they had struggled for centuries to do for themselves. It seemed too much to believe that on Calvary's cross Jesus Christ had done everything necessary to give those who believed on Him right standing with God.[6] (See Romans 9:30-33.)

To summarize the argument to this point, ethnic Jewishness does not suffice to identify a person as one of God's children. God extends His mercy to all, but some reject it. God knows in advance who this will be and, if it suits His purpose, He can reveal it in advance and declare what He will do in response. Since God has no obligation to show mercy to anyone, His extension of mercy to some longer than to others is no basis to accuse Him of being unjust. When people stand before God in judgment, none—including Esau and Pharaoh—will be able to say that God did not extend His mercy to them or that He treated them unjustly. All have the opportunity to respond to God in faith. Those who do will receive faith's reward; those who do not will suffer the consequences.

Ignorance of God's Righteousness

The desire and prayer of Paul's heart was the salvation of national Israel (Romans 10:1; see also Romans 9:3.) Apart from faith in Jesus Christ, Jewish people—like all others—are not saved, regardless of how zealous they may be (Romans 10:2).

As a people, the Jews attempted to establish their right standing with God by adherence to the law of Moses, rather than by faith in God (Romans 10:3-5).[7] But right standing with God has always, in every age, come by faith in God. It does not result from what people can do, but from what God has already done. (See Romans 10:6-8.) Genuine faith begins in the heart and is exhibited in one's words. (See Romans 10:9-13.) Calling on God for salvation must be preceded by believing, and believing must be preceded by hearing a proclamation of the gospel. (See Romans 10:14-18.)

Provoking Israel to Jealousy

By a series of quotations from the Hebrew Scriptures, Romans 10:19-21 explains why God turned to the Gentiles as a consequence of His rejection by national Israel: "But I say, did Israel not know? First Moses says: 'I will provoke you to jealousy by those who are not a nation, I will anger you by a foolish nation.' But Isaiah is very bold and says: 'I was found by those who did not seek Me; I was made manifest to those who did not ask for Me.' But to Israel he says: 'All day long I have stretched out my hands to a disobedient and contrary people.'"

The first quote is from Deuteronomy 32:21. Since Israel rejected the Messiah, God would provoke them to jealousy by those who are "not a nation," (i.e., Gentiles). In a poetic turn, Romans repeats the essence of the statement by declaring God will move Israel to anger by "a foolish nation." This God did by extending salvation to the Gentiles apart from the law of Moses or identification in any way with national Israel. (See Romans 11:11.)

The second quote is from Isaiah 65:1. Here, it points out that the Gentiles, who were not seeking Israel's God, found Him. He manifested Himself to those not asking for Him. This quotation gives Old Testament support to Romans 9:30.

The quote from Isaiah 65 continues, with reference to verse 2. Israel is the object in this verse; it was national Israel to whom the Lord stretched out His hands all day long. They were a disobedient and contrary people. The identification of Isaiah 65:2 as being addressed "to Israel" underscores that in Romans 10:19-20 the reference is to Gentile nations.

In sum, although God sovereignly elected national Israel (Romans 9), the nation is now under divine rejection because of their rejection of the Messiah. But in spite of their present spiritual darkness, Israel has a bright hope. God will turn to them in the future and deal with them on the basis of the new covenant. That is the message of the next section of Romans.

Israel's Future Salvation

Since national Israel is presently under a state of rejection from God due to their failure to accept the promised Messiah, does this mean there is no hope for the nation in the future? First-century readers understood that individual Jewish people could be saved even though the nation as a whole was apostate, but what does the future hold, if anything, for the nation?

God's temporary rejection of national Israel does not translate into rejection of individual Jewish people: "I say then, has God cast away His people? Certainly not! For I also am an Israelite, of the seed of Abraham, of the tribe of Benjamin" (Romans 11:1). Paul himself was Jewish, and he could trace his ancestry back to Abraham through the tribe of Benjamin. Thus Paul was living proof that God had not "cast away His people." Any individual Jew can be saved even though the nation has temporarily lost its special status with God.

Again, Romans uses the strong denial: *me genoito*. If we translate *me genoito* as "may it never be," the idea is not only that God has not to this point cast away His people, but that He will never do so. God will yet fulfill every unconditional promise He has made to the nation.

Paul's ability to identify his tribe disproves the speculations about "ten lost tribes" and the claims of British Israelism that whites in Great Britain and America are somehow Jews from these "ten lost tribes." The mention of the "twelve tribes" in James 1:1 also argues against any concept of "lost" tribes. Representatives of all the tribes were in the number who returned to Jerusalem for the rebuilding of the city and Temple under Ezra, Nehemiah, and Zerubbabel,[8] and in several places the New Testament identifies Jews by their tribe of origin. Anna was of the tribe of Asher (Luke 2:36), Mary and Joseph of Judah (Matthew 1:3; Luke 3:33), and Paul of Benjamin (Philippians 3:5). Revelation 7 describes the sealing of 144,000 Jews during the Great Tribulation, 12,000 from each tribe. The term "the twelve tribes" refers to all of ethnic Israel.

"God has not cast away His people whom He foreknew. Or do you not know what the Scripture says of Elijah, how he pleads with God against Israel, saying, 'LORD, they have killed Your prophets and torn down Your altars, and I alone am left, and they seek my life'? But what does the divine response say to him? 'I have reserved for Myself seven thousand men who have not bowed the knee to Baal'" (Romans 11:2-4). We must understand this reference to the foreknowledge of God in the context of the earlier use of the term. (See Romans 8:29.) He knows if an individual will eventually come to Him, and He will not turn away from any such person so as to make the individual's salvation impossible.

For an illustration, this passage appeals to the story of Elijah when he cried out in desperation, thinking he was the only person left in Israel who was faithful to God. (See I Kings 19:10-18.) The believing Jews in Rome may have had a similar question since the vast majority of national Israel had rejected the Messiah. But God's answer to Elijah was that He had a remnant of seven thousand people in Israel who were still faithful to Him. Likewise, there was a remnant in national Israel who believed on the Messiah.

The Present Remnant

"Even so then, at this present time there is a remnant according to the election of grace" (Romans 11:5). Since

God selected Abraham and his descendants through Isaac and Jacob, there has never been a time when none of them had faith. Even during times of gross spiritual darkness, there were always those who retained their faith in God. It is no different during this era, when national Israel has rejected the Messiah and is thus out of favor with God. There is a remnant who does believe on Jesus. This remnant is made up of those who respond to the grace of God by placing their faith in the Messiah, Jesus Christ. To believe on Jesus is not a work that gains favor with God, for the ability to believe is itself a gift of God. (See Romans 11:6; Acts 15:7-11; John 20:30-31.)

National Israel Failed to Obtain Her Goal

Israel as a nation did not obtain the right standing (righteousness) with God she sought by the law of Moses.[9] There was a remnant within national Israel—the elect (Romans 11:5)—who obtained right standing with God because they believed on the Messiah Jesus and put their trust in Him through His blood. The rest, because they rejected the Messiah, were blinded to the only means of obtaining right standing with God.

Romans 11:8 combines Deuteronomy 29:4 and Isaiah 29:10: "Just as it is written: 'God has given them a spirit of stupor, eyes that they should not see and ears that they should not hear, to this very day.'" Because of national Israel's rejection of the Messiah, God has given them a "spirit of stupor." They are unable to see and hear. (See Isaiah 6:9-10.) Their current spiritual dullness does not result merely from lack of information; their spiritual insensitivity stems from their refusal to believe on Jesus as their promised Messiah.

To further support this point, Romans 11:9-10 quotes the Septuagint translation of Psalm 69:22-23: "And David says: 'Let their table become a snare and a trap, a stumbling block and a recompense to them. Let their eyes be darkened, that they may not see, and bow down their back always.'" To the Hebrews, the "table" represented the blessing of God, the richness of His provisions. The greatest blessing God gave to national Israel was the promised Messiah. But since Israel rejected their greatest blessing, all other blessings—specifically, the Hebrew Scriptures (Romans 3:2), their special standing as a nation, the long-absent Shekinah, the covenants, the law of Moses, and the priesthood (see Romans 9:4)—became a snare, a trap, and a stumbling block. In essence, national Israel rejected her greatest blessing in favor of lesser blessings, so the lesser blessings themselves became a source of "recompense" to them. The things that once were sources of blessing to them now became a source of pain.

The history of national Israel from her rejection of the Messiah demonstrates the truth of this statement. The penalties for violation of the Palestinian covenant provide the most dramatic and accurate description of their troubles. (See Deuteronomy 28:58-68.) Since a chief purpose of the old covenant was to bring national Israel to the Messiah (Galatians 3:24), those who rejected their Messiah thus rejected the very purpose of the old covenant itself. At that point, the curses associated with the old covenant asserted themselves in the most forcible way; once people rejected the God-given function and purpose of the old covenant, its blessings were no longer operative. All that remained for Israel were the curses. (See Galatians 3:10, 13.)

With the rejection of the Messiah and the new covenant He instituted (Matthew 26:28), Israel's spiritual vision was darkened and their backs were bowed down. Their rejection of Jesus Christ resulted in spiritual insensitivity and servitude to the Gentile nations of the world. (See Luke 21:24.)

Israel's Fall Is Not Permanent

In recognition of the apparent hopelessness of the spiritual condition of national Israel, Romans 11:11 asks, "I say then, have they stumbled that they should fall? Certainly not! But through their fall, to provoke them to jealousy, salvation has come to the Gentiles." Since national Israel is now in a state of spiritual stupor because they "stumbled" at that "stumbling stone" by rejecting their Messiah, does this mean that they have fallen permanently? (The Greek word translated "fall" in the first part of the verse, *pesosin*, refers to a fall that is permanent.) Again we find the strong denial: *me genoito*. But through the temporary fall (here the Greek word is *paraptomati*, which refers to a temporary fall) of national Israel, salvation has been extended to the Gentiles to "provoke [Israel] to jealousy."

A brief statement then reveals the restoration to favor with God that will come to national Israel and the impact it will have on the Gentile nations of the world: "Now if their fall is riches for the world, and their failure riches for the Gentiles, how much more their fullness!" (Romans 11:12). A great deal of theological truth is summed up in this significant verse.

If the temporary stumbling of national Israel has resulted in "riches for the world" (i.e., salvation through the Jewish Messiah being offered to Gentiles, Romans 11:11), *how much more* will Israel's fullness result in riches for the world (i.e., Gentiles)? The "fullness" is the nearly universal conversion of the Jewish nation that will occur when they embrace Jesus Christ as their Messiah. (See Revelation 7:3-8; Zechariah 12:10.) At this point Jesus will establish His new covenant with Israel (Jeremiah 31:31-34), and the ultimate outpouring of the Holy Spirit will transpire (Joel 2:28-32). The knowledge of the Lord will be universal, and there will be no need for people to be taught (Jeremiah 31:34; Isaiah 11:9; Habakkuk 2:14).

This final restoration of national Israel will result in riches for the Gentiles, even though the church age will already have ended with the rapture of the church (I Thessalonians 4:13-18; 5:1-9). At this point all the Old Testament prophecies about salvation coming upon the Gentiles through the influence of the redeemed nation of Israel will be fulfilled.

The salvation now enjoyed by Gentiles is a mystery the Hebrew prophets did not foresee (Ephesians 3:1-6). The Hebrew Scriptures foretold the salvation of Gentiles, but they did not reveal the removal of ethnic distinctions between Jews and Gentiles in the church age. (See Ephesians 2:11-22; Galatians 3:28; Colossians 3:11.) The yet unfulfilled prophecies about Gentile salvation are tied to the restoration of national Israel to God's favor. (See Isaiah 11:6-16; 49:5-6; 54:1-3.)

Blindness in Part

Romans 11:13 begins to address Gentile readers directly. Paul wished "by any means" to "provoke to jealousy" those who, like Paul, were ethnically Jewish in order to "save some of them" (Romans 11:14). The casting away of national Israel resulted in salvation being offered to Gentiles, but when the Jewish people turn to Jesus as their Messiah, it will be as great a miracle (Romans 11:15). Since the father of the Jewish nation, Abraham, was holy (separated unto God), so is the nation (Romans 11:16).

The Abrahamic origin of ethnic Israel is represented by a cultivated olive tree (Romans 11:24). Some of the natural branches, which represent those Jews who rejected Jesus, have been broken off from the tree. In their place were grafted Gentiles who did believe on Jesus (Romans 11:17). This was no cause for the believing Gentiles to boast; their privilege was by faith only, and if they failed to believe, they would lose their place just as did the unbelieving Jews (Romans 11:18-22). On the other hand, God will graft back into the cultivated olive tree any Jew who believes on Jesus (Romans 11:23-24).

Spiritual blindness is not universal in Israel: "For I do not desire, brethren, that you should be ignorant of this mystery, lest you should be wise in your own opinion, that hardening in part has happened to Israel until the fullness of the Gentiles has come in" (Romans 11:25). Paul resorted to a phrase he used often: he did not wish his readers to be ignorant. (See Romans 1:13; I Corinthians 10:1; 12:1; II Corinthians 1:8; I Thessalonians 4:13.) Paul was on a divine campaign to remove ignorance and to enlighten people as to God's purposes and ways. In this case, he wished to make clear to his Gentile readers a "mystery," that is, something previously hidden but now made known. The mystery not revealed in the Hebrew Scriptures is that partial spiritual blindness is upon Israel "until the fullness of the Gentiles has come in." The blindness is partial in that it affects only those Israelites who reject Jesus as the Messiah. It is temporary in that it will last only until the full number of Gentiles has been grafted into the holy olive tree.

National Israel does have a future that will be inaugurated in conjunction with the end of the present (church) age, during which God is visiting "the Gentiles to take out of them a people for His name" (Acts 15:14).

This statement does not imply that no Gentiles will be saved after the church age. Gentiles who come to Jesus the Messiah after the church age will not, of course, be part of the church; they will fulfill Old Testament prophecies concerning the salvation of Gentiles in conjunction with the restoration of national Israel to favor with God, which begins during the Great Tribulation (Revelation 7) and continues throughout the Millennium.

All Israel Will Be Saved

At the termination of the church age, God will turn His attention again to national Israel, and many Jewish people will place their faith in Jesus, their promised Messiah. "And so all Israel will be saved, as it is written: 'The Deliverer will come out of Zion, and He will turn away ungodliness from Jacob; for this is My covenant with them, when I take away their sins'" (Romans 11:26-27). "All Israel" refers to the nation as a whole. Not every ethnic Jew will be saved; every ethnic Jew who has faith in Jesus Christ will be saved. (See Romans 9:6.) The true Jew at any given time is the one who believes on Jesus as the Messiah.

Romans quotes from Isaiah 59:20-21 and 27:9 to indicate that at this time God will establish the new covenant with Israel. (See Jeremiah 31:31-34; Ezekiel 36:24-28.)

The Deliverer is Jesus the Messiah who will "turn ungodliness from Jacob" (Ezekiel 20:34-38) and forgive the sins of those who believe on Him. He will forgive sins on the basis of the blood He shed. (See Luke 22:20; Revelation 7:14.)

Beloved Enemies

In order for God to offer salvation to Gentiles under a different arrangement than the Hebrew Scriptures revealed, He had to deal with national Israel as His enemy; that is, He had to break off from the holy olive tree those who rejected the Messiah. "Concerning the gospel they are enemies for your sake, but concerning the election they are beloved for the sake of the fathers. For the gifts and the calling of God are irrevocable" (Romans 11:28-29).

But this does not mean God actually hates individual Israelites. Indeed, for the sake of the fathers (Abraham, Isaac, and Jacob), He loves them. Even though many Jewish people turned away from Jesus, the nation is elected of God so that God may yet fulfill all the promises He made to the fathers. God does not fail to keep His unconditional promises, nor does He revoke any unconditional call He has made. The Abrahamic covenant is unconditional. Even the unfaithfulness of national Israel cannot prevent God from keeping his promises to Abraham.

It is important to note here that some of God's promises are conditional; some callings are conditional. The Edenic, Mosaic, and Palestinian covenants were conditional. The Davidic covenant had both conditional and unconditional elements. The Adamic, Noahic, Abrahamic and new covenants are unconditional.[10] God will never fail to keep any promise He has made unconditionally, nor will He fail to keep any conditional promise He has made when the conditions have been met.

Still speaking directly to Gentiles, Romans 11:30-31 says, "For as you were once disobedient to God, yet have now obtained mercy through their disobedience, even so these also have now been disobedient, that through the mercy shown you they also may obtain mercy." Just as Gentiles had once been disobedient to God but were now recipients of God's mercy due to the disobedience of many Israelites, so by the demonstration of God's mercies upon Gentiles many Israelites will again turn to God. This is another way of saying that God intends the salvation of Gentiles to "provoke them [Israel] to jealousy."

Romans 11:32 presents a wonderful example of how God uses human sinfulness to demonstrate His glory: "For God has committed them all to disobedience, that He might have mercy on all." Due to Israel's disobedience, God counts them as sinners; thus His salvation is an act of mercy. God knows that the Jewish people can never gain right standing with Him by their own efforts, so He will deal with them on the basis of mercy, not the works of the law. This is how God has dealt with all of humanity.

Confirming the Promises

Romans 15:9 declares the validity of the Jewish claim to a unique relationship with the Messiah: "Now I say that Jesus Christ has become a servant to the circumcision for the truth of God, to confirm the promises made to the fathers." The Messiah's special relationship to the Jewish people ("the circumcision") rests upon His commitment to keep the promises God made to the fathers: Abraham, Isaac, and Jacob.

Notes

[1]See Craig S. Keener, *The IVP Bible Background Commentary: New Testament* (Downers Grove, IL: InterVarsity Press, 1993), 412.

[2]See discussion under "Can the Uncircumcised Be Righteous?" in chapter 1.

[3]Paul's statement that his conscience bore him witness may give us some insight into the significance of Jesus' statement in John 8:18: "I am One who bears witness of Myself, and the Father who sent Me bears witness of Me." Some people, not fully realizing the significance of the Incarnation in terms of the unfragmented deity manifest in the person of Jesus Christ, insist that Jesus' statement here indicates that the Father is a person distinct from the Son. To them, for Jesus to bear witness of Himself demands that He be one person, and for the Father also to bear witness of Him demands that the Father be another person, in view of Jesus' statement in John 8:17: "It is also written in your law that the testimony of two men is true." If this is the way we are to understand Jesus' statement, the following questions immediately come to mind: (1) Are the Father and Son two individuals as radically separate as two men are? (2) If the Father and Son are two persons in the Godhead, they would be equally God and absolutely one in will, mind and purpose. How valid, then, would it be to call upon both of them to witness? Since there is no possibility their witness could disagree under any circumstance, is this really the equivalent of the witness of two independent people who could disagree, given the right circumstances?

Jesus was, of course, a genuine human being and, in the mystery of the Incarnation, at the same time genuinely God. If Paul, who was nothing but a human being, could declare that his conscience bore him witness without suggesting that his conscience had distinct identity from him, surely Jesus could declare that the Father was His witness without suggesting that the Father was thus a distinct person from Him. To suggest that the Father and Son are as radically distinct as two human beings is surely to press the anthropomorphic language of Scripture beyond its legitimate bounds. If this is what Jesus meant in John 8:17, we shall have to redefine the meaning of monotheism; there would be, after all, two individuals, both of whom are known as "God" and both of whom could offer separate and independent testimony.

But that is not Jesus' meaning. His claim to bear witness of Himself is testimony to the genuineness and completeness of His humanity; His claim that the Father bears witness of Him is testimony to the genuineness and completeness of His deity. Though there is, and forever will be, a mystery here, Jesus' own words demonstrate the validity of this assessment. When the Pharisees asked Him, "Where is Your Father?" Jesus answered, "You know neither Me nor My Father. If you had known Me, you would have known My Father also" (John 8:19). The Pharisees' question was an excellent opportunity for Jesus to explain His relationship to the Father, if indeed the Father was a person distinct from Him. Instead, Jesus declared that the Pharisees did not know Him *or* His Father; if they had known Him, they would have known His Father as well. In other words, knowing the Father is bound up in knowing Jesus; the Father cannot be known apart from knowing Jesus. The Pharisees did not understand the Incarnation; they certainly knew Jesus as a human being. What they did not know is that He was at once both God and man. If the Incarnation meant that Jesus as a second person of the Godhead was manifest in the flesh, the Pharisees could theoretically have understood that and still not have known the Father, if the Father was the first person in the Godhead. But since Jesus is God Himself manifest in the flesh, to know Him is to know God fully; to know Jesus is to know the Son (God as He is manifest in the Incarnation) and the Father (God in His transcendence). Jesus' testimony of Himself arose out of His humanity; the testimony of the Father arose out of His deity.

[4]See discussion under "The Law Belongs to Israel" in chapter 3.

[5]See discussion under "Faith's Companions: Hope and Love" in chapter 4.

[6]See discussion under "Pursue Right Standing with God by Faith" in chapter 4.

[7]See discussion under "The Righteousness of Faith" in chapter 4.

[8]Under Zerubbabel, representatives of the tribes of Judah, Benjamin, and Levi, together with many others—apparently of a variety of tribes—whose spirits God had quickened, returned to the land (Ezra 1:5). Ezra was a Levite, and with him other Levites and "some of the children of Israel" returned (Ezra 7:7). When the rebuilt Temple was dedicated, sacrifices were offered "according to the number of the tribes of Israel" (Ezra 6:17). This number was twelve. Those offering the sacrifices included "the priests, and the Levites and the rest of the descendants of the captivity" (Ezra 6:16). This, and the dedication's being made on behalf of all twelve tribes strongly implies that representatives from all the tribes were present. Although this return was from the Babylonian (southern kingdom), not Assyrian (northern kingdom), captivity, there were representatives of all twelve tribes in the southern kingdom at the time of the captivity who had chosen to live there rather than to identify with the idolatry of the northern kingdom (II Chronicles 11:16).

[9]See discussion under "Pursue Right Standing with God by Faith" in chapter 4.

[10]See discussion under "Advantages of Being Jewish" in chapter 6.

Gentiles:
Showing the Favor
Of God to All People

Since the church at Rome was made up of both Jewish and Gentile believers, the Book of Romans addresses both. Although believing Jews and Gentiles share a commonality of faith and doctrine, it is important that each understand the other's role in the current work of God during the church age. It is apparent that tension existed between these groups of believers at Rome, and not without reason.[1] But if all believers, regardless of ethnic origin, could grasp the message of Romans, the tensions would dissipate. God loves Jews and Gentiles equally, though each has a specific place in His plan.

English translations of the Book of Romans tend to use three words to refer to non-Jews: "Gentiles," translated from the Greek *ethnos*; "nations," also translated from *ethnos*; and "Greek," from the Greek *hellen* (from which is derived "Hellenism," a reference to culture arising from the syncretism of Greek culture and the various cultures of the peoples conquered by Alexander the Great).

Paul's Ministry to the Gentiles

In his salutation, Paul identified his personal ministry as extending to the Gentiles: "Through whom we have received grace and apostleship for obedience to the faith among all nations for His name" (Romans 1:5). (See Acts 9:15.) To the Jews, any reference to the "nations" was a reference to Gentiles. Only Israel was the chosen "nation." (See Psalm 33:12; 147:20.) God sent Paul to the Gentiles to bring them to "obedience to the faith," a reference to the content of the gospel.

Paul's desire to visit the Romans was not a sudden impulse. He had long wanted to visit them but had always been hindered previously. He wished to have some "fruit" among the Roman believers, just as he had among the many Gentile churches he founded and ministered to. Contextually, the "fruit" he had in mind are people who responded to his preaching of the gospel to come to Christ for salvation. (See Romans 1:13.)

Paul recognized his personal responsibility to preach the gospel to all, including the "Greeks," those in the Roman Empire who had adopted the Greek language and the Hellenistic culture, and the "barbarians," those in the Roman Empire who had not done so. "I am a debtor both to Greeks and to barbarians, both to wise and to unwise" (Romans 1:14). The "wise" were those educated in Greek philosophy; the "unwise" were those who had not studied the currently prevailing "wisdom."

The universal nature of Paul's commission serves as a useful pattern for all whom God calls to preach the gospel.

Though, like Paul, we may have a specific calling to a particular cultural or language group, we bear a larger responsibility to declare the good news about Jesus Christ to everyone without regard to social or cultural status.

With everything in him, Paul was ready to preach the gospel in Rome: "So, as much as is in me, I am ready to preach the gospel to you who are in Rome also" (Romans 1:15). As the capital of the Roman Empire, this vast city seethed with the variety of people described in the previous verse: the cultured, Greek-speaking, "wise" citizens of the Roman Empire and the "barbarians" who had retained only their native tongues and who had not troubled themselves to adapt to the Greek influences on society at large.

Paul's statement that the gospel of Christ was for the Jew first simply means that, historically, it was offered to the Jewish people before it was offered to the Gentiles.[2]

Gentiles Do Not Have the Law

In keeping with the testimony of the Hebrew Scriptures that God gave the law of Moses exclusively to the nation of Israel, Romans 2:14-15 says, "For when Gentiles, who do not have the law, by nature do the things contained in the law, these, although not having the law, are a law to themselves, who show the work of the law written in their hearts, their conscience also bearing witness, and between themselves their thoughts accusing or else excusing them." This passage speaks of the testimony of conscience, one of the ways God has given general revelation[3] to all humanity.

No Gentile had all the commandments of the law of Moses written on his conscience, however. General revelation does not include the vast multitude of special commandments God gave to Israel under the law (e.g., the Sabbath day, holy days, the wearing of tassels with a blue thread running through the center, the ban on plowing with an ox and a donkey together, etc.). Conscience reveals only the most general of moral codes. Neither does any Gentile actually keep perfectly the law of conscience, for the Gentile's conscience both accuses and excuses him. In other words, the Gentile is accused by his conscience when he violates it; he is excused by his conscience when he acts in accordance with its scruples. The point is that Gentiles, who do not have the law, are still guilty of sin when they violate their conscience, just as surely as Jews sin when they violate the written Law (Romans 2:12).

Why Gentiles Blaspheme the Name of God

In a rebuke of Jewish elitism, Romans 2:24 states, "For 'the name of God is blasphemed among the Gentiles because of you,' as it is written." This verse quotes the Septuagint translation of Isaiah 52:5. This is an interesting example of the use of the Old Testament in the New Testament. In many cases, various New Testament writers quote the Old Testament to demonstrate the fulfillment of specific prophecies. But in other cases, like here, they take Hebrew Scriptures that in their original context are far removed from New Testament events and under divine inspiration apply them to those events.

In the original context, the words quoted here recount Israel's captivity in Egypt, then their oppression by Assyria, and looked ahead to the captivity of Judah in Babylon. The Hebrew text of the portion of Isaiah 52:5 quoted here is translated, "And My name is blasphemed continually every day." Romans, however, quotes the Septuagint's rendering, which is a freer translation. Contextually, the meaning of the Hebrew text includes "among the Gentiles because of you," for Isaiah's discussion concerned the Babylonian captivity and thus the blasphemy that the Babylonians would utter against Israel's God as a result of their disdain for the Jews.[4]

The use of Isaiah 52:5 reminds Jewish readers that their inconsistencies dishonor the God who gave them advanced revelation. The Gentiles were aware of the Jews' claim to superiority of knowledge, and when they saw the Jews' failure to abide by their own law, it prompted the Gentiles to mock the revelation received by the Jews and the God who gave it.

Gentiles Judging Jews

Jews referred to Gentiles as the "uncircumcised." Their lack of circumcision meant they were outside the covenant God made with Israel. Although the Jewish people did receive superior revelation, they were intrinsically no better than the Gentiles, for if a Gentile kept "the righteous requirements of the law" (Romans 2:26), it would be irrelevant that he was uncircumcised. God would treat him as if he were circumcised. Indeed, if a Gentile did fulfill the law, he would be in a position to judge the Jews who broke it (Romans 2:27).

This argument does not mean any Gentile was successful in keeping all 613 commandments of the law of Moses. Since the larger context of these verses shows that all—Jews and Gentiles—are sinners who "fall short of the glory of God" (Romans 3:23), the statement here must be hypothetical.[5] But this does not weaken its point. The

Jews who boasted because of superior revelation (Romans 2:17-20) needed to realize that there was no benefit from merely having the law; the benefit was in keeping it. If any individual Gentile kept requirements of the law that any individual Jew did not, his being outside the covenant would be of no consequence. He would be in a position to judge the disobedient Jew.

Jews and Gentiles Are of the Same Value to God

The superior revelation of the Jewish people and their being part of the chosen nation did not mean they were better than Gentiles. The reason is that all—Jews and Gentiles—are sinners. (See Romans 3:9.) It is not the recipient of revelation who benefits from the revelation, but the person who is obedient to the revelation. Inherently, no human being is better than any other.

The God of All People

The only way the Jewish people could claim ethnic superiority over the Gentiles would be if the God of the Jews were exclusively an ethnic god who was superior to all other ethnic gods. But this is not so. There is only one God, and He is not the God of the Jews alone. He is also the God of the Gentiles. (See Romans 3:29.)

The thing that contributes value to a person is the identification of his God. A person severed from God is bereft. But when a human being has a direct link to the heavenly realm, he takes on eternal value. Since Gentiles and Jews both worship the same God, they are of equal value. And whether one is a Gentile or Jew, he is justified by faith in God (Romans 3:30).

The Father of Many Nations

Abraham's justification prior to his circumcision guarantees that he is the father not just of believing Jews, but first of believing Gentiles. (See Romans 4:9-12.) This is how God has fulfilled His promise to make Abraham the father of *many nations.* (See Romans 4:16-18.) Physically, the promised seed was isolated in Isaac and then in Jacob. But Abraham was to have other descendants in addition to his promised physical seed. These other descendants included believing Gentiles from many nations of the world. (See Galatians 3:29.)

Vessels of Mercy

We see the equality of Jews and Gentiles during this era in that both are the recipients of "the riches of His glory," both are "the vessels of mercy," and both are "called." (See Romans 9:23-24.) To support the equality of the Jews and Gentiles, Romans 9:25-26 quotes Hosea 2:23 and 1:10: "And He says also in Hosea: 'I will call them My people, who were not My people, and her beloved, who was not beloved.' And it shall come to pass in the place where it was said to them, 'You are not My people,' there they shall be called sons of the living God."

Here is an interesting example of the use of the Old Testament in the New Testament. In their original context, these verses refer not to Gentiles but to unbelieving Israelites who were not—at the time—living as the people of God. But under the inspiration of the Holy Spirit, Paul used these words in a new context to show that the Gentiles would be called the people of God.

Once again, we see that God takes the initiative in showing mercy. If the idea of unconditional election were true, it would seem God would be obliged to call *all* Gentiles His people, because *all* of them were formerly not His people. In other words, if God determined to call as His people those who were not His people, this would include all Gentiles of the world. But, just as "they are not all Israel who are of Israel" (Romans 9:6), so the only Gentiles whom He will call His people are those who respond in faith to His mercy.

On the basis of their faith in Jesus Christ, Gentiles attain right standing with God (Romans 9:30). Since the only way for Jewish people to attain right standing with God is by faith, "there is no distinction between Jew and Greek, for the same Lord over all is rich to all who call upon Him" (Romans 10:12).

Jealous of a Foolish Nation

God intends to use the salvation of the Gentiles to provoke Israel to jealousy: "But I say, did Israel not know? First Moses says: 'I will provoke you to jealousy by those who are not a nation, I will anger you by a foolish nation.' But Isaiah is very bold and says: 'I was found by those who did not seek Me; I was made manifest to those who did not ask for Me'" (Romans 10:19-20). These quotes, from Deuteronomy 32:21 and Isaiah 65:1, underscore that God extends salvation to Gentiles without regard to the law of Moses and without requiring Gentiles to identify with national Israel, whether by circumcision or proselytization. This would certainly provoke to jealousy those who thought they were superior to the Gentiles due to the superior revelation they had received.[6]

Romans 11:11 continues the theme of Israel being provoked to jealousy by the salvation of Gentiles. But then Romans 11:12 points out that though the failure of national Israel to believe on Jesus the Messiah did result in spiritual riches for the Gentiles, even greater riches will result for all the nations of the world when Israel does come to faith in Jesus.[7]

A Message for the Gentiles

Romans 11:13-15 begins to address Gentile believers directly: "For I speak to you Gentiles; inasmuch as I am an apostle to the Gentiles, I magnify my ministry, if by any means I may provoke to jealousy those who are my flesh and save some of them. For if their being cast away is the reconciling of the world, what will their acceptance be but life from the dead?" Since Romans clearly declares that the Jews' ethnic background and special revelation does not gain them any salvific advantage, there was a danger the Gentiles would denigrate their Jewish brethren and belittle their heritage. God had called Paul to be an apostle to the Gentiles (Acts 9:15; Galatians 1:16; 2:7-8; Ephesians 3:8), and he asserted his authority to make these statements.

Paul hoped that by bringing Gentiles to enjoy the privileges of faith in the Jewish Messiah he could "provoke to jealousy" his Jewish brethren in order to save some of them. (See Romans 10:19; 11:11 and 9:1-3; 10:1.)

In a statement similar to Romans 11:12, verse 15 reiterates that if Israel's temporary stumbling resulted in Gentiles ("the world") being reconciled to God, their return to favor with God (conditioned upon their acceptance of Jesus Christ as their Messiah) would be nothing short of "life from the dead." The implication is that Israel's spiritual "resurrection" will be a miracle.

The reconciliation of the world to God does not mean that all Gentiles will be saved, but that the barrier to fellowship with God was removed by the Atonement. Individual Gentiles must still act on the provisions of the Atonement in order to receive its benefits. (See II Corinthians 5:18-20.)

Romans 11:17-18 continues to speak directly to Gentiles: "And if some of the branches were broken off, and you, being a wild olive tree, were grafted in among them, and with them became a partaker of the root and fatness of the olive tree, do not boast against the branches. But if you boast, remember that you do not support the root, but the root supports you." Abraham was the root of the holy olive tree, and the branches were his natural offspring, the Israelites. The failure of some of Abraham's offspring to believe on Jesus as their Messiah resulted in "some of the branches" being "broken off." It is important to note that not *all* the branches were broken off; this would imply God's rejection of every individual in national Israel. The only branches that were broken off were those who did not believe (Romans 11:20, 23).

In this analogy, Gentile believers—a "wild" olive tree—were grafted into the holy olive tree to replace those branches that had been broken off. Gentile believers have thus become partakers "of the root and fatness of the olive tree," which means they enjoy a blessing associated with the Abrahamic covenant. (See Romans 4:9-11.)

The Abrahamic blessing extended to Gentile believers does not include the specific promises intended for Abraham's physical seed only, such as the land promises. Believing Gentiles enjoy a far more significant blessing: justification by faith. This is, at least in part, what is meant by the words "In you all the families of the earth shall be blessed" at the establishment of the Abrahamic covenant. (See Genesis 12:3.) A person does not have to be a physical descendant of Abraham to enjoy this blessing.

Romans warns Gentiles not to "boast against the branches." Just as Jewish believers must not boast in the superiority of the revelation they had received (see Romans 2:17; 3:27), so Gentiles must not boast that they had replaced Jews as recipients of the blessing of Abraham (justification by faith). Gentile believers are to keep in mind that this blessing springs from the root—Abraham—not from the Gentiles themselves.

Gentiles need to consider not only the goodness of God in grafting believing Gentiles into the "root and fatness of the olive tree" (Romans 11:17), but also His severity in cutting off the unbelieving Jews (Romans 11:22). The only way Gentiles can retain their place in the olive tree (the Abrahamic blessing of justification by faith) is to "continue in His goodness," by continuing in faith. If God would cut off Israelites because of their unbelief, He will certainly cut off Gentiles for the same reason. (See Romans 11:19-21.)

The idea of unconditional eternal security cannot be reconciled with Romans 11:20-22. Clearly, continued faith in Jesus Christ is necessary for continued placement in the olive tree.

Romans 11:24 underscores and reiterates everything previously said on the subject at hand: "For if you were cut out of the olive tree which is wild by nature, and were grafted contrary to nature into a cultivated olive tree, how much more will these, who are natural branches, be grafted into their own olive tree?" Gentile believers have been taken from a wild (noncovenantal [see Ephesians 2:12]) olive tree and grafted into the tree that represents the Abrahamic covenant. If this, a seeming impossibility, could be done, it is even more likely that natural descendants of Abraham will be grafted back into the Abrahamic covenant if they believe.

Romans 11:30-31 still addresses Gentiles directly: "For as you were once disobedient to God, yet have now obtained mercy through their disobedience, even so these also have now been disobedient, that through the mercy shown you they also may obtain mercy." Just as the Gentiles had once been disobedient to God but were now recipients of God's mercy due to the disobedience of many Israelites, so by the demonstration of God's mercies upon Gentiles many Israelites will again turn to God. This is another way of saying that God intends for the salvation of Gentiles to "provoke them [Israel] to jealousy." (See Romans 10:19; 11:11.) Since both Jews and Gentiles are sinners, God deals with all of them on the basis of mercy (Romans 11:32).

The Unsearchable Judgments of God

Since the Gentile nations of the world failed to live up to general revelation (see Romans 1:18-32), God chose Abraham, a man of faith, to establish a new nation to be His special people. But since Abraham's descendants failed to live up to special revelation (see Romans 2:1-29), God returned to the Gentiles to save them on the basis of mercy (Romans 11:32), not works. When He has accomplished this purpose (Romans 11:25), He will turn again to Israel, this time dealing with them on the basis of mercy, not the law of Moses.

One might ask why God did not do this in the first place. But His plan illustrates the "depth of the riches both of the wisdom and knowledge of God." His judgments are "unsearchable" and His ways "past finding out." (See Romans 11:33.) This passage uses the words of the Septuagint translation of Isaiah 40:13 and gives a free rendering of Job 41:11 to underscore that the mind of God is unknown to man; God does not seek counsel from any human being. No one has first given to God so that God must repay him.

This last point summarizes the reason God has done things as He has. *It is so that nobody, Gentile or Jew, could ever say he had earned his right standing with God.* If any Gentiles had lived up fully to general revelation, or if any Jews had lived up fully to special revelation, they could boast in their good works. They could claim that they had first given to God (by being perfectly obedient) and that their salvation was what God had repaid them for their achievements. But the human inability to live up to general or special revelation has destroyed the possibility of this kind of boasting (Romans 1-3). Humans can boast only in God. (See Romans 3:27.)

God Will Be Glorified by Gentiles

One of God's purposes for the Messiah's ministry was to provide a means for the Gentiles to glorify God for His mercy. Since the Messiah performed a unique Jewish ministry (Romans 15:8), Gentile believers could not disparage their Jewish brethren. But since there was also a Gentile component to Jesus' ministry, Jewish believers could not discount their Gentile brethren.

Romans 15:9 quotes the Septuagint translation of II

Samuel 22:50, from David's song of deliverance, to indicate the willingness of Israel's greatest king to identify with Gentiles: "And that the Gentiles might glorify God for His mercy, as it is written: 'For this reason I will confess to You among the Gentiles, and sing to Your name.'" David was willing to confess to God and sing to the name of God *among the Gentiles*; he stood in solidarity with the Gentiles. He stood among them, as one of them, joining with them in their praise and worship to God. If David could do this during the Mosaic covenant, surely Jewish believers under the new covenant can do the same.

Romans 15:10 quotes Deuteronomy 32:43 from the song of Moses to underscore further the privilege Gentiles have to join together with the Jews in their praise of God: "And again he says: 'Rejoice, O Gentiles, with His people!'" If Moses, the deliverer of Israel from Gentile (Egyptian) captivity, invited the Gentile nations of the world to join Israel in the praise of Israel's God, Jewish believers in the church, who are one in Christ with their Gentile brethren, can surely accept them as equals in worship. If Moses exhibited no prejudice even during the Sinaitic covenant, surely Jews and Gentiles can put aside their ethnic differences under the new covenant. There is a practical point here: Worshiping together is a great equalizer of people.

Romans 15:11 adds another quote to the argument for Gentile equality, this time from Psalm 117:1: "And again: 'Praise the LORD, all you Gentiles! Laud Him, all you peoples!'" Even during the law of Moses, Gentiles were invited to praise Yahweh, the God of Israel. God would accept their praises as readily as those of Israel. Thus, there was no basis for Jewish people to claim superiority.

In this bit of Hebrew poetry from Psalms, the second

line repeats the meaning of the first. "Praise the LORD, all you Gentiles," is the same as, "Laud Him, all you peoples."

The final appeal to the Hebrew Scriptures to demonstrate the equality of Gentiles with Jews is a form of the Septuagint version of Isaiah 11:10: "And again, Isaiah says: 'There shall be a root of Jesse; and He who shall rise to reign over the Gentiles, in Him the Gentiles shall hope'" (Romans 15:12). Jesse was David's father, and Isaiah describes the Messiah as arising from David's lineage. (See Psalm 132:11; Acts 2:30.) The passage from which Romans quotes anticipates the salvation of Gentiles during the Millennium. (See Isaiah 11:6-9.) Romans does not claim the complete fulfillment of this prophecy in the church; it offers this insight from Isaiah to support the thesis that the Messiah is available equally to Gentiles and Jews. He will reign over Gentiles as surely as He will reign over the restored nation of Israel. The Gentiles will find their hope in the Messiah as certainly as the Jews will.

The Offering of the Gentiles

Paul desired to "be a minister of Jesus Christ to the Gentiles, ministering the gospel of God, that the offering of the Gentiles might be acceptable, sanctified by the Holy Spirit" (Romans 15:16). Apparently he wanted to remind Jewish readers of this letter that the salvation of Gentiles resulted from God calling Paul as a minister to the Gentiles. There was thus no reason for Jewish believers to reject their Gentile brethren. If the Gentiles were acceptable to God, they should certainly be acceptable to Jewish Christians. The sanctification of the Gentiles by the Holy Spirit rendered illegitimate any reason a Jewish believer may have had to reject the Gentiles.

261

Things Christ Accomplished
To Make the Gentiles Obedient

Paul made it his aim not to glory in anything or anyone other than Christ Jesus: "Therefore I have reason to glory in Christ Jesus in the things which pertain to God. For I will not dare to speak of any of those things which Christ has not accomplished through me, in word and deed, to make the Gentiles obedient—in mighty signs and wonders, by the power of the Spirit of God, so that from Jerusalem and round about to Illyricum I have fully preached the gospel of Christ" (Romans 15:17-19).

The phrase "the things which pertain to God" is identical to that in Hebrews 2:17. Both are translated from the Greek *to pros ton theon*. Romans uses the phrase to refer to Paul's ministry to the Gentiles; Hebrews uses it to relate to the Messiah's ministry as our High Priest. Both uses suggest to knowledgeable Jewish readers that the priesthood of the old covenant was no longer in force; the current sacrifices were not those of the Mosaic code. In terms of the new covenant, "the offering of the Gentiles" is a sacrifice to God.

The only things Paul dared to mention were those things Christ had accomplished through him to bring the Gentiles to the point of obeying the gospel. (See II Thessalonians 1:8.) Even though Paul discussed himself, his ministry, and his plans for the future, he was careful not to claim personal responsibility for the good things accomplished among the Gentiles; all of them are the work of God.

Christ accomplished the conversion of the Gentiles through Paul "in word and deed," "in mighty signs and wonders, by the power of the Spirit of God." Paul's ministry was not limited to the vocal declaration of the gospel; it included the confirmation of the Word with signs following. (See Mark 16:17-20; Acts 13:11; 14:3, 8-10, 19-20; 19:11-12; 20:9-12; 28:1-8; I Corinthians 2:1-5; II Corinthians 12:12; Hebrews 2:3-4.)

Nothing in Scripture suggests that God limited this kind of ministry to the first century. The New Testament everywhere confirms that for the gospel to be "fully preached," or declared in its fullness, both components are required: the vocal declaration of the Word and the confirmation of the Word with signs following. (See Acts 2:22, 43; 4:29-30; 5:12.)

Everywhere Paul went, "from Jerusalem and round about to Illyricum," his ministry was characterized by signs and wonders. No doubt, as indicated in John's record of the ministry of Jesus (John 20:30-31; 21:25), Paul did many miraculous things not recorded. There is no biblical record of his ministry in many areas, yet he indicated that everywhere he went, mighty signs and wonders accompanied his ministry.

The phrase "and round about" means literally "and in a circle." Paul had ministered from Jerusalem and its environs all the way to Illyricum. His ministry from the home of Christianity to its farthest reaches in his travels was consistent in having signs and wonders.

This is the only place in Scripture that mentions Paul's ministry in Illyricum. Illyricum is also known as Dalmatia, and the area corresponds to the present Yugoslavia, Bosnia-Hercegovenia, and Croatia. If one draws a straight line from Jerusalem to Illyricum, the distance is about nine hundred miles. Paul, of course, traveled a circuitous route.

The Gentiles' Duty

In discussing a contribution Gentile believers in Macedonia and Achaia made to the poor Jewish believers in Jerusalem, Paul wrote, "It pleased them indeed, and they are their debtors. For if the Gentiles have been partakers of their spiritual things, their duty is also to minister to them in material things" (Romans 15:27). The gift the Gentile believers sent by Paul to the poor believers in Jerusalem was a freewill offering ("it pleased them indeed"). The Gentile believers viewed themselves as debtors to the Jewish believers, for the Gentiles had partaken of the Jews' "spiritual things" and considered it their duty to minister to the Jews in "material things." Galatians 6:6 also mentions this principle. (For the Gentiles' participation in the "spiritual things" of the Jews, see Romans 11:11-12, 17-18; 15:12; Galatians 3:14; Ephesians 3:6.)

The detailed discussion of the empathy Gentile believers elsewhere had for Jewish believers no doubt strengthened the appeal to Jewish and Gentile believers in Rome to lay aside their differences and unify around the person of Jesus Christ. The generosity of the Gentiles would serve as an example to Gentile believers in Rome to have concern for the welfare of Jewish brothers; the humble acceptance of Gentile assistance by the poor Jewish believers in Jerusalem would serve as an example to Jewish believers in Rome to be humble in their relationship with the Gentiles.

The Gratitude of the Gentile Churches

As he began his final remarks to the believers in Rome, Paul extended gratitude to Priscilla and Aquila, his "fellow workers in Christ Jesus" (Romans 16:3). This

Christian couple had risked their necks for Paul's life, but he was not the only person who was grateful to them. So also were "the churches of the Gentiles" (Romans 16:4). Priscilla and Aquila have a high profile among New Testament believers. (See Acts 18:2, 18, 26; I Corinthians 16:19; II Timothy 4:19.)

Paul met Aquila and Priscilla on his second missionary journey in Corinth. They were fellow tent makers who had left Rome for Corinth due to Claudius's decree expelling all Jews from Rome. (See Acts 18:2.) When Paul left Corinth, they went with him (Acts 18:18), remaining in Ephesus when Paul left that city (Acts 18:19). During their time in Ephesus they showed Apollos "the way of God more accurately" (Acts 18:26). When Paul returned to Ephesus on his third missionary journey, they ministered to him again and sent their greetings to the church in Corinth (I Corinthians 16:19). They had moved back to Rome by the time Paul wrote this letter; later they returned to Ephesus (II Timothy 4:19). Aquila and Priscilla are examples of a couple who gave themselves without reservation to the work of the Lord, supporting themselves all the while by a trade.

We do not know when Priscilla and Aquila risked their lives for Paul's sake. Whenever it was, they must have protected him from some danger while endangering their own lives.

Aquila and Priscilla had a "church in their house" in Rome, as they also did while in Ephesus (I Corinthians 16:19). Recent archeology supports the New Testament suggestion that the church often met in houses of believers. The Jewish people frequently converted houses into synagogues. The same was true of the first-century Christians and churches. Most of the congregations Paul founded held meetings in the houses of individual members.[8] But the evidence suggests that they soon converted these houses into full-fledged church buildings:

> One of the most impressive discoveries . . . comes from Dura-Europos, a Roman garrison on the Euphrates River in what is now Iraq, dating to before 256 C.E. On one street was a house that had been renovated, in three stages, into a sanctuary of Mithras, a Persian god whose cult spread throughout the Roman Empire from the second half of the first century C.E. onward. Farther down the same street, another house had been converted, in two stages, into a synagogue. Its assembly hall contained one of the earliest datable Torah niches, and on its walls were elaborate frescoes depicting stories from the Hebrew Scriptures. Farther down the same street was a house that was renovated to become a Christian church, with a small assembly hall and a room set aside for baptism.[9]

Rome itself offers evidence of houses or apartments being adapted for use as churches: "More evidence of religious pluralism in the Diaspora can be seen in Rome. Excavations beneath several basilicas, such as those of St. Clement and SS. John and Paul, reveal earlier buildings—houses or apartment complexes—that were being renovated for religious use as early as the first century."[10]

Though we do not know precisely why the Gentiles owed a debt of gratitude to Priscilla and Aquila, it may be that some of them had worshiped in their home.

The Revelation of the Mystery

Romans 16:25-27 records the final words to the believers in Rome: "Now to Him who is able to establish you according to my gospel and the preaching of Jesus Christ, according to the revelation of the mystery which was kept secret since the world began but now has been made manifest, and by the prophetic Scriptures has been made known to all nations, according to the commandment of the everlasting God, for obedience to the faith— to God, alone wise, be glory through Jesus Christ forever. Amen."

God is able to establish believers according to the gospel. (See Romans 1:1, 9, 15-16; 2:16.) Paul closely associated the gospel with the "preaching of Jesus Christ." The gospel is, in essence, the declaration of the good news about the salvation found in Christ Jesus.

The "mystery which was kept secret since the world began," but now revealed and operative in the church, is "that the Gentiles should be fellow heirs, of the same body, and partakers of his promise in Christ through the gospel" (Ephesians 3:6). (See also Ephesians 3:1-5; Colossians 1:26-27.) The Hebrew Scriptures had anticipated the salvation of Gentiles, but only in conjunction with the restoration of the nation of Israel in the kingdom age. This has not yet occurred. (See Romans 11:12.) In the present "mystery" form of the kingdom, the ethnic distinctions between Jews and Gentiles are of no significance. (See Galatians 3:28; Colossians 3:11.)

This reference to the "mystery" is appropriate in a letter that to a large degree seeks to restore unity between Jewish and Gentile believers. Since it is in the conclusion, no doubt it is a matter of great importance.

From the perspective of the New Testament, it is clear that the "prophetic Scriptures," the Hebrew Scriptures, contain many direct prophecies, shadows, and types of the Messiah. (See Luke 24:44-45; John 5:39; Romans 1:2; Hebrews 10:1; Colossians 2:16-17.) But the prophets themselves did not fully comprehend the significance of what they wrote. (See I Peter 1:10-12.)

The Hebrew Scriptures do not directly predict the church age. Now that the mystery had been revealed, however, the Hebrew Scriptures could be and were used to preach Christ "to all nations, according to the commandment of the everlasting God, for obedience to the faith."

"The commandment of the everlasting God" is apparently the great commission given by Jesus. (See Matthew 28:19-20; Mark 16:15; Luke 24:47; Acts 1:8.) If so, this statement is a strong affirmation of the deity of Jesus Christ.

Notes

[1]See opening discussion in chapter 6.

[2]For comments on Romans 1:16 and 2:9-10, see discussion under "To the Jew First" in chapter 6.

[3]"General revelation" refers to the universal revelation of God in creation (Psalm 19; Romans 1:19-20) and conscience. Some scholars also include history. "Special revelation" refers to the specific revelation God has given in the Scriptures and in the person of Jesus Christ.

[4]See the discussion of the use of the Septuagint in the New Testament in note 19 on pages 60-61.

[5]The phrase "if an uncircumcised man keeps the righteous requirements of the law" is in the third class condition. The Greek language of the New Testament presents conditional sentences in four classes, ranging from first class to fourth class. The first class condition affirms the reality of the condition, i.e., it assumes that the condition is being met. The second class condition is contrary to fact, which affirms that the condition is not being met. The third class condition affirms that the condition is not presently being met; it is the probable future condition. But context is still the deciding factor in matters of grammar. Since Romans 1-3 affirms that no one, Jew or Gentile, lives up fully to the revelation he has received, Romans 2:26-27 cannot mean there actually will be Gentiles who will perfectly obey the law of Moses.

[6]See discussion under "Provoking Israel to Jealousy" in chapter 6.

[7]See discussion under "Israel's Fall Is Not Permanent" in chapter 6.

[8]Eric M. Meyers and L. Michael White, "Jews and Christians in a Roman World," *Archaeology*, March/April 1989: 31.

[9]*Ibid.*, 32.

[10]*Ibid.*, 33.